Beautiful New Sky

Beautiful New Sky

Fabricating Bodies for Outer Space
in East Germany's Military Laboratories

INES GEIPEL

Translated by Nick Somers

polity

First published in German as *Schöner neuer Himmel. Aus dem Militärlabor des Ostens* © 2022 Klett-Cotta – J. G. Cotta'sche Buchhandlung Nachfolger GmbH, gegr. 1659, Stuttgart

This English translation © Polity Press, 2024

The translation of this book was supported by a grant from the Goethe-Institut.

Polity Press
65 Bridge Street
Cambridge CB2 1UR, UK

Polity Press
111 River Street
Hoboken, NJ 07030, USA

ISBN-13: 978-1-5095-5999-2 – hardback

A catalogue record for this book is available from the British Library.

Library of Congress Control Number: 2024935057

Typeset in 11 on 14pt Warnock Pro
by Cheshire Typesetting Ltd, Cuddington, Cheshire
Printed and bound in Great Britain by CPI Group (UK) Ltd, Croydon

The publisher has used its best endeavours to ensure that the URLs for external websites referred to in this book are correct and active at the time of going to press. However, the publisher has no responsibility for the websites and can make no guarantee that a site will remain live or that the content is or will remain appropriate.

Every effort has been made to trace all copyright holders, but if any have been overlooked the publisher will be pleased to include any necessary credits in any subsequent reprint or edition.

For further information on Polity, visit our website:
politybooks.com

Contents

Acknowledgements

My thanks go first to Jacob, without whom this book would not have been written. Jacob is not his real name, but his story is authentic.

The research for this book was complex. I should like therefore to thank the archivists at the Freiburg Military Archive, the Federal Archive in Berlin, the archive of the Academy of Sciences in Berlin, the State Archives in Schwerin, the State Archives in Rudolstadt, the Stasi Documents Authority in Schwerin and the library of the German Aerospace Centre in Berlin-Adlershof for making available archive documents, for pointing me in the right directions and their friendly assistance.

Once again I should like to thank my publishers for their belief in the idea of the book, for their support and material and practical generosity. Above all my thanks go to my editor Tom Kraushaar, my proof-reader Christine Treml, naturally Katharina Wilts, Verena Knapp, Marion Heck and everyone at Klett-Cotta who made this book possible in the first place.

And as ever nothing would have been possible without friends. I thank Eva-Maria Otte for helping with the arduous search for material, for her initial proofreading, her precise ideas, her tweaking but also for her dramaturgical reliability.

I thank Andreas Petersen for his love, for his care and his moral support. I thank Rena Krebs for her time and indefatigable support. I thank Gerit Decke for her inspiration and long friendship. And I thank Dorit Linke for our runs in the Volkspark and her constant encouragement.

IG, February 2022

The emotional state of a person can be assessed on the basis of the timbre and volume, speech tempo, choice of words and sentence structure. The aim of the 'speech' experiment is to assess the subject's functional state under real flight conditions by examining the frequency and amplitude characteristics of GDR cosmonauts when pronouncing the number '226' in German (in the transcription 'zwo sechsundzwanzig'). The 'speech' experiment is intended to further perfect the medical monitoring of cosmonauts' health status in flight.

BArch (Berlin), DY 30/69605, p. 89, unnumbered

Unknown soldier

Dual text. 26 April 2018. The day began like days that you can't ever forget often do: normal, bright, sunny. In Berlin. A normal sky, normal coffee. I had to go into the city. A press conference was scheduled for 11 o'clock. On the podium three women. They were going to tell their stories. I was the moderator and was prepared accordingly.

Today is 26 April 2021. Exactly three years ago, something entered my life. That's what people say looking back. I clearly remember standing at the front of the stage during the press conference. In the room were a large number of media representatives. To my right, the three women. At some point I stepped back two or three paces so that I could see them from behind. As if their backs would also speak, I thought. As if it were possible to be in front and behind at the same time. As if the two were distinct from one another. A kind of dual text. The women spoke of abuse and violence in sport. Calmly, clearly, forcefully. At least that's what it must have sounded like in the room. They said what they had to say. The journalists asked their questions. It sounded like a completely normal press conference.

26 April 2021. I am sitting at the kitchen table and start writing this down. I think about a report. The first image is the

backs, the second the e-mail I received twelve hours after the press conference. I have it in front of me. It says: 'OK, sweetie, you've had your fun. Much too long, in our opinion. Now it's our turn and it won't be fun. No stone will be left unturned. You can bank on it. U.S.'

I sometimes get e-mails that start with 'sweetie'. Hello, sweetie, or listen, sweetie, or hey, sweetie. I print them out and keep them in a special binder. As far as I'm concerned, they are eyewitness accounts. The sweetie mail of 26 April 2018 had the e-mail address unknownsoldier@ – and didn't end up in the binder. It remained on my desk. Unknown soldier. It was evidently meant to sound important, some kind of secret mission. But what was to be made of it? Was someone trying to frighten me? And why? Wasn't it going a bit far? When I think back to the situation today, I imagine Gerhard Richter's cloudy pictures. Blurred, out of focus, without clear contours. But perhaps there's no need for a picture. Perhaps I should just try to write down what happened.

The *unknown soldier*. It called to mind the grave of the unknown soldier in Canberra that I visited years ago. All the red flowers on the wall. They were poppies. Later I thought of camouflage dress, lowered visors, and my father. Almost fifteen years working for Department IV of the State Security, military training, spy, border crosser, West agent with eight different identities. He was the unknown soldier in my head. But was that necessary just because of another stupid e-mail? I hesitated. The thing with the East. It hadn't got any easier over the years. Something had come back, shifted, moving in an endless loop. At least that's how I felt. Twenty years ago it had seemed sorted, with dissertations, detailed research and investigation. But now it was as unsettled as ever. Slippery, vague, bottomless. More and more the East looked as if it were being questioned out of existence, rewritten, filtered out, reinterpreted.

If you ask people who know about it, they speak strangely of a Restoration, but they seem tired of it all. What remains of a country and a system that no longer exists? What was its core? What is its legacy if not just personal memories? And why unknown soldier? Who wanted to make their presence felt again? My gaze rested on the two letters U.S. Strange. More so, because the unknown soldier was evidently alluding to what had been occupying me for some time.

Pneumatic. I always have my Mac with me when I travel. That way I can reconstruct fairly well where and when I was in a particular institution, office or archive. According to the computer, in the week before 26 April 2018, I was in the military archive in Freiburg. I like going there. The days in that place are somehow pleasantly ritualized: the entrance door matt white, metal, matter-of-fact. The pneumatic sound, delicate, scraping. A cold suction noise as it closes. Click. I have to pass a checkpoint and them I'm inside.

That April three years ago was hot, the Freiburg reading room a refrigerator. I had socks with me. The files I wanted were on the checkout counter. The man who slid them towards me smiled kindly. I took the pile. Was that the beginning? There was a term I'd had in my head for some time: military-industrial complex, known in German as MIK. During the GDR days we had often joked about it. When we passed a Russian barracks, we said MIK. Whenever there was the silvery smell of radiation, we called it MIK. Restricted areas, black holes in the system – that was MIK. What did it mean? Who could we have asked?

Polytrauma. In 1989 MIK was gone. Disappeared, like so much else? But somehow MIK was stuck inside me and had a life of its own. Virtual Eye, the bionic brain GPS, Sea Hunter, the Mars cities planned by NASA – whenever I heard or read something to do with military and research, these three letters came into my mind like flashes of light. At some point I thought that whatever it was, it was material that was worth looking into. And also, how come we know so little about it? Or am I the only one who knows nothing about it? That's why I decided to go to Freiburg. If there was anything to find out about MIK, that would be the place. I looked on the Internet and discovered that Freiburg was where everything to do with the GDR military research complex, or at least what was left of it, was kept. Documents on Bad Saarow Military Medical Academy and the Central Military Hospital, Königsbrück Institute of Aerospace Medicine, Stralsund Navy Medicine Institute, the Academy of Sciences, the Interkosmos programme. Holdings transferred to the Freiburg Military Archive from the Bundeswehrkommando Ost, which only existed from October 1990 to June 1991. MIK. Like investigating an imprecise memory, something that had always been there without ever being questioned. An obsolete fantasy, a relic of the Cold War, a conspiracy theory? Perhaps it had rather to do with what is inside us. With the bloodhound of history, which picks up the scent and trots off because that's what it does, with its nose to the ground.

The air conditioning clanks. In front of me the files, the catalogue numbers. I look out of the window. Where am I? In April 2018. A bank of early summer clouds drifts gracefully past the archive window. I think of temptation, inertia, overview and distance. I'm sitting over fragile pieces of paper. Archives are strange places. In effect time capsules. Someone shuts out the here and now, draws you down a long corridor, hangs around for a while and then stops in front of something that happened in the past but hasn't found its place. It's still on its way, not yet landed.

On my order list for the archive week in April 2018: 'clinical picture and treatment of selected sabotage poisons', 'consequences of ionizing radiation on tissue', 'new findings on panic in battle', 'placenta research', 'medical preparation of cosmonaut candidates', 'psychiatric aspects of suicide attempts by prisoners', 'blood substitutes', 'performance-oriented uses of women', 'polytrauma'.[1] Items in the digital ordering system that caught my eye. But where to start? With sky. Definitely there. With the question of habitable zones and extraterrestrial life. With something that is bigger, older, more infinite than anything we can imagine. Isn't there something that exists even without us?

Isolation chamber. 'Human beings remain the most universal, flexible and important component of a control system, whereby an effectively coordinated distribution of functions between humans and machines improves the reliability of the overall system.'[2] This is the first sentence of the postdoctoral thesis by Hans Haase, an aerospace medicine specialist born in 1937, from the Institute for Aerospace Medicine in Königsbrück, just a few kilometres from Dresden. The institute, a facility of the National People's Army (NVA), was answerable to the Ministry of National Defence. Haase was its deputy director and sometime chair of the Cosmic Biology and Medicine working group[3] within the Interkosmos programme. He also supervised Major General Sigmund Jähn, the first German in space, who orbited the Earth in summer 1978. Haase defended his cosmonaut thesis in November 1988. During the intervening ten years, not only in Königsbrück, there was a 'systematic study of aerospace medicine projects', as stated in the minutes of a meeting of the Leibniz Sozietät der Wissenschaften zu Berlin in 2008.[4]

A system within a system that was systematically researched. What was that about? Space travel is the ultimate heroic project, complete with smiling photos and a good portion of national pride. Perhaps it's the rigid spacesuits, the anachronistic outfits, which have somehow always prevented me from taking all of the space exploration images seriously. Lots of waving from the capsule, floating gently in space, wide-legged hops on the moon. As if watching an ecstatic group of people fooling around in nowhere land, protected only by the universe. But what were we actually seeing?

Haase's cosmonaut study offers a precise date for a reality check: 1 October 1976. On that day, seven men – the shortlist following a tough selection procedure involving three hundred GDR military pilots – travelled to the Königsbrück Institute of Military Medicine. In the following weeks, each of them was to undergo a battery of personal hyper-tests. They were to be examined for physical fitness, technical knowledge, spatial orientation, motor skills, in other words their general suitability for space travel. After the hard weeks of testing, only four of them were sent to Star City near Moscow. In the end, just two remained: Sigmund Jähn and Eberhard Köllner. They became research cosmonauts and underwent a two-year special training programme: days spent in a soundproof isolation chamber, flight training on a MiG-21, flight simulators, special training in a chamber heated to 60 degrees Centigrade, reduced-gravity aircraft, training in a human centrifuge, training at high altitude, autogenic training, endless theoretical classes.[5]

Were they happy about it? Did they feel special? What was it like to be in an isolation chamber for days on end? What kind of body was going to be catapulted into space? I hear portholes, chambers, capsules closing and something getting inside me. People are walking outside on the pavement in front of the Archive. I can hear their footsteps, their voices, their laughter and think of the cheeriness of life. Inside, in the file, are the years 1976, 1977, 1978. Quiet years in the East. It was crumbling. You could hear it. I lived in a boarding school in the Thuringian Forest. When we returned after the summer holidays in early September 1976, Claudia, my friend at the time from Zeitz, talked about the Lutheran pastor Oskar Brüsewitz, who two weeks earlier had doused himself with petrol and set himself alight on the square in front of his church. A public display that left its mark. We lay in our beds and spoke about the burning man, his 'No' in our loud silence.

Source texts. A file is a file and initially nothing more than a chance find. If it is to be relevant sometime later for anything, it needs points of references. Source texts, contexts, a fabric in which the individual document begins to speak with others, with time, with other events. It needs a leitmotif, a mental space. Memory is not so simple, however. We tend to reshape the past in hindsight. We would like to have been the ones with the big white bows, the guardians of ambitious dreams. The cheerful ones, the strong, the leaders. We would like to have dared to stuff ourselves with worms, known how to dive head first and tussle with the boys. Hindsight doesn't like to move in circles but prefers to tell heroic stories. But how to identify what really happened, how to confront it, tease it out, inter-rogate it? And what does it mean? Is it necessary? Absolutely. The abandoned legacy of the East has still not found a home or points of consensus. There are, no doubt, many reasons for this. What is still lacking is the historical context. What is lack-ing is a perception of the weight of experience after over fifty years of dictatorship. And despite assurances to the contrary, the necessary research is still missing. Does anyone seriously believe that we're over it, that we can put it behind us?

I was just sixteen years old when the aeronautic medicine specialist Hans Haase investigated weightlessness in his 1976 cosmonaut study. I know where I was at the time, what I was doing, what I wanted and what I had already become. To put it another way, I can't read the Freiburg files objectively. I'm part of it, the investigation of the time, the material, the unex-plained, the silence in the relationships. That's how it is and it can't be changed. Over forty years have elapsed between 1976 and 2018. Even a short while ago I would have said that that's a long time. But what sources, what contexts, what history are we so sure about that it can't be questioned?

Everything, from the beginning. I was reminded of Jacob. A few weeks earlier, perhaps in January 2018, he had spoken to me after an event in Berlin. For five years I had been chairperson of Doping-Opfer-Hilfe, an organization that supports athletes who had been part of the dark side of sport. Mostly victims of the official doping in the GDR. What was seen and heard when the floodlights were turned off and in the time after the major competitions cannot be talked about in public. It's not relevant. Sport is about winning, a world religion without a god, or whatever. But please don't spoil the programme for all the spectators sitting in their homes. Sport is nice, sport is good, sport is for everyone. And the rest? Shrug the shoulders, bad luck, your own fault. Dark afterimages are not nice. It's best if they don't appear in the first place.

Jacob and his restless eyes, the faded jeans, the baseball cap with NY on it. His way of coming straight to the point, of taking me over to a table and starting to unpack his photos. His time as a circus acrobat. Here, he points proudly, that was me. On the photo a fine-limbed body, swinging high up under the dome of the big top. On the other side, two hands ready to catch him. Then one time it went wrong, he said, looking at me steadfastly. And then? – It was over. I was too scared and started racing.

His time as a cyclist and the next stack of photos. And certificates. And medals. I took that just as seriously as my time in the circus, he assured me. I nodded and studied him more closely for the first time. Why are you here? I asked. Jacob explained. I was in the forecourt of Dresden train station. A car arrived. We drove for almost an hour. We got out and I spent the next ten weeks in a room next to Sigmund Jähn. – Next to Sigmund Jähn? The first German cosmonaut? The man with the baseball cap pushed more photos across the table as if they would prove something. He was on one of the photos, very young, with a laurel wreath around his neck, his face sweaty and beaming. When was that? – 1974. – I mean with Sigmund Jähn? – Oh, also around that time. But I only realized it later when he kept on waving at me on the television from his space capsule.

Jacob's eyes, his body, thin as a rake. He spoke of needles, wires, biopsies. Are you sure they did something to you? A question I needn't have asked. That's why he was here. He shook his head. There's nothing, no records. I looked at his face. I'd been doing it for over five years: research, conversations, authorities, archives, at the end almost nothing, at least nothing of importance, nothing incriminating, nothing that could help someone like Jacob. It's not about you, he broke the silence. What then? – I need to know. I need to know about the programme, everything, from the beginning. – They did something to you, you say? – Yes. – And now you want to know what they did because you're not well?

We both looked at the same spot on the floor as if it could pull us out of this situation. Jacob took off his baseball cap. Not a hair on his head, no eyelashes, no eyebrows. You're not interested, are you, he said dismissively. But that's not even the point. It's about fighting the void. That nothing is being done, no explanations, no one who will talk. As if it never happened. – But couldn't it have been different? – How so?

Anaemic. 'The special characteristics of space travel,' says the Haase study, are 'weightlessness, cosmic radiation, artificial living space, nervous and emotional tension'.[6] Longing for the forests, I would have thought, or fear perhaps. But in fact I'd never really thought about it. Weightlessness for me was a trampoline or roller coaster, an elusive feeling of flying, something inevitably to do with the air. Now I read that in weightless conditions the muscles lost their strength and the blood rushed to the head. That it caused a 'negative water balance' and 'acute deterioration of visual acuity'.[7] Energy consumption under weightless conditions was also five times greater.

As if our earthly bodies in space took a blow to the system. Particularly muscles, bones, blood, brain. As if we headed in the sky towards a profound state of physical dementia, I thought. And added to that, being forced to stay in a hermetically sealed room, to arrange oneself in a tightly confined space, to shut down one's body. For weeks, months, even years. It was also incredibly loud in the capsule, apparently. The machine worked continuously. The inside of the spacesuits was cold. Because the eyes don't become heavy, it's almost impossible to sleep. Day and night cease to exist in space. And finally the stress of ionizing radiation, flashes of light, 'sensory hunger'.[8]

The air conditioning is struggling. I'm sweating. I hadn't imagined it like that. The fact that you can't move. Blood, bones, muscles, brain going haywire. No sleep, intensive radiation, utter boredom. Haase's investigation makes the particular drama of the cosmic hero more like a bizarre theatrical spectacle.

Terra incognita. Five days after the first sweetie e-mail came the second one. 'Hey, sweetie, are you getting worried? Don't worry, we haven't forgotten you. Just a couple of details to clear up. It's all about the fine-tuning, as they say. U.S.' Mails of this type often come in series. So it wasn't really surprising. And yet, there was something. Something in the words, the tone. As if I somehow recognized where the words were coming from. *Unknown soldier.* Like in a Sunday evening police thriller without an ending, a shady figure with a black hood pulled over his face. The detective murmurs mystifyingly about someone who has been living in the city for a long time, maybe a refugee from the Bosnian war or Afghanistan. An old soldier who knows his trade. Someone in the shadows who has learned from scratch how to work quietly. A social outlaw who prefers to remain hidden.

What do cosmonauts eat? Most of the food is like on Earth. There are seventy products available, packed in portions, with 65 per cent in dehydrated form. Eating from tubes is already a thing of the past in manned space flight. The only products still in tubes are fruit juices or concentrates, puree and paste-like items. This is because of the special features of food intake under weightless conditions. No crumbs or drops of fluid can be allowed to escape into the cabin atmosphere, because if inhaled they could lead to serious complications.

Zentrales Archiv des Deutschen Zentrums für Luft- und Raumfahrt e.V., Göttingen, BAAR, A872, unnumbered.

The New Man

Sense of wellbeing and total experience. What did Jacob have to do with Sigmund Jähn? Did I have something to do with the unknown soldier, and if so, how come? Where was the link? Today, three years later, these questions are no longer relevant. In April 2018, however, I was completely in the dark. All I had was the cosmonaut study. And I was stuck there.

'Humanity is taking the first steps towards overcoming geocentrism as the prevailing and historically conditioned world view of humanity,' it says on page 23. It continues by asserting that it is a question of 'overcoming organ-based thinking'.[1] But what would that look like? Were the organs placed neatly side by side and only lined up in front of the worn-out heart for the daily briefing?

The New Body and the various concepts promoted in the past century. A lot has been said about this. I'm talking about the new perceptions and new realities of the individual within the new collective. In every case there must have been a specific date and location for the laboratory assistants and designers in the various research complexes. They will have sat down, discussed and thought about the issues. The most important decisions, as in most cases of this sort, will not have been written down. And then, what happened next?

'One day you can tell all this to anyone who is willing to listen. No one will believe you.'[2] A line from the film *The Serpent's Egg* by Ingmar Bergman. I saw it in autumn 1980 in Jena. I was twenty years old at the time. I can still recall what I felt as I watched it, or rather the fact that I didn't want this feeling. As if something was getting too close to me. The images, the nervousness, the excessiveness, the swirling. 'Through the thin membranes, you can clearly discern the already perfect reptile.' This sentence seemed to me like a code, just as the entire film was evidently conceived as a code. Life as if in a cocoon, the walls, the mirrors, the cameras behind them. It was a mild evening when I came out of the cinema. I waited at the bus stop and took the bus to a satellite community near the autobahn. Something in me preserved the film like a canned product, like a place in my mind.

Words are sometimes so delicate that they want to dissolve. The thin membrane. We look back from the present to the previous century. We would like to have been special, balanced, well-disposed, gentle. But how to make out the thin membrane in all this, how to defend it, how to keep on resisting it at all? The New Man and Communism. That was my starting point. That's where I come from. The desire afterwards to talk about it as accurately as possible from the very beginning. There probably wasn't a precise starting point. The fear of not being able to talk about it accurately enough, of not getting it right. Communism as utopia, promise, illusion, myth, madness, crime. Communism as reality. As a concrete experience in time, as a concrete life in a particular place, as a perception, as a feeling, as a physical sensation. What it means in principle for all of life to be controlled from a single centre. In return, every thought, every movement, every feeling in society was directed towards it. The world as a total experience.

I am sitting in Freiburg and looking at the 1970s in the East. The time oozes out of the words. It still tastes today of utopian innocence. Better, more cheerful, more peaceful, more unified. More progressive. A dense rhetorical forest. What is between the words and not expressed in the letters is also there. But what does it signify? And above all, what does it mean today? As if the reality could be pushed beyond the limits of the words.

The 1970s. We wore bell-bottoms, platform shoes and surreal hairstyles. Biermann's expatriation in 1976 and Charter 77 in Prague a year later. And, finally, August 1978 and Sigmund Jähn in space. An unparalleled propaganda coup. While the first German orbited the Earth 125 times, compulsory military training was introduced in all schools in the country. Girls now also learned how to shoot. They marched, threw hand grenades, tackled assault courses with gas masks, rescued their fellow pupils from burning bunkers. Later, before lights out in the military camp, we turned our boots at the end of the bed towards the West. We lay awake and waited for the camp commander's shrill whistle in the corridor. It told us that we were about to go on a night-time run to throw back the enemy.

State trauma. The week in Freiburg. The press conference just a few days later. A normal day in Berlin. I drove to the university, met friends, worked in the Doping-Opfer-Hilfe advice centre. The second Compensation Act was in full swing. I was thinking of Jacob and everything about him. Johanna with the nervous blotches on her face, who sent us a letter every three months in which she wrote that there was a crack in her life that couldn't be papered over. Karla, now a successful senior doctor in Leverkusen, who overnight couldn't run anymore and spent the evenings crying in the gymnasiums of her childhood. My role was to listen and just to be there.

The major trial of those responsible for the official GDR doping programme took place in 2000 in Berlin. Twenty former female athletes and one male athlete testified and were questioned in court. I was one of the co-plaintiffs. The first Compensation Act covered almost 200 former athletes; with the second law there were almost 2,000. Numbers are numbers. But between them is a wound. It can only tell its story, stutteringly, partially, sketchily. It has to overcome many holes and obstacles. And yet this wound just got bigger over the years.

After the fall of the Berlin Wall, there were drawn-out investigations, then lots of research, trials, sentences, ultimately compensation. At first it was about understanding and scandal, but then the focus shifted increasingly to those who had been used by the system. The question of what the compulsory official doping did to people's lives, the violence, abuse, dependence, destabilization. These facets gradually became better known. I regarded it as my job to help make a political issue of this physical state trauma, to draw attention to it and to ensure that it was not forgotten.

Radiating bodies. But where did the official physical conditioning in the East come from? What was behind it? What ideas, what hopes, what realities? The New Man as an anthropological dream loop, as a constantly transforming hope, as a great exculpatory narrative. Healing through renewal, solace through nature, much vitalist manna, the belief in the true society, the ultimate escape project. It was in this optimistic mood that a shaky Europe set out in the twentieth century and transformed its old belief in the afterlife into social utopias in the here and now. In particular, the two political religions – Nazism and Communism – based their promise of salvation on Christian traditions, which they fed into their radicalizing programmes.

'Part of the dynamism of totalitarian movements is that the ambitions, ideas and interests behind them are not static socioeconomic preconditions but point forward into a no-man's land of ill-defined promises and expectations,' wrote the historian Gerd Koenen in his book *Utopie der Säuberung*.[3] But the dark side of history cannot be retold in terms of initial expectations, hopes or futures. Words are afraid, probably just as much as we humans. They also have to cross an unbridgeable gap and overcome what Koenen describes as a 'cruelly failed experiment'.[4] They would probably prefer to avoid the issue, to be left in peace, to roll up, close the shutters and doze off for a while. But they are there to listen. They have to capture, record and settle time. And? Is that not precisely their problem?

The biopolitical utopias in Russia didn't need the revolution in 1917 as an initial shock. Their beginnings go much further back and read like a fascinating collection of the most diverse theoretical stories. In *Philosophy of the Common Task*, written in the late nineteenth century, Nikolai Fyodorov (1829–1903), a contemporary of Tolstoy and Dostoyevsky, proposed a bold deal between the past and the future, or more precisely between all living and dead beings, to unify them in an 'eternal universe'. He claimed that Western civilization with its prosperity, success and hunger for power could be managed only through 'supramoralism'. He was referring to socialism as the paradise on Earth.[5] Mankind would have to do this in a 'joint work of total mastery and transformation of the universe, combating and overcoming death and the reawakening – full resurrection – of all the dead'.[6] The main actor in his concept of immortality was none other than a 'self-regulating artificial body'.[7] There was no need for a soul, because the world in any case existed only in a purely material physical form. To that extent, it was no problem either to manipulate the New Body through technology.

Present-day transhumanists must have enjoyed reading Fyodorov's tracts. He was already an inspiration and guiding figure in his day, particularly for his disciples. One of them was Konstantin Tsiolkovsky (1857–1935), who dreamed of space towers with elevators into the sky, of interstellar colonies, of the metamorphosis of all mankind into a gigantic 'radiating body'. He built the first wind tunnel in Russia and a centrifuge for cockroaches and chickens, conceived a steerable metal airship, sought to establish contact with the inhabitants of other planets, designed multi-stage rockets with liquid fuel, and made plans for manned space stations. Evidently a jack-of-all-trades, who was promoted after the Revolution first by Lenin and then by Stalin as a 'visionary son of the people' and potent propaganda legend.

Collective experiment. The interplanetarianist ideas were so popular among the Russian intelligentsia that it didn't take much to promote them even further in the heat of the Revolution. Advocates wanted to belong to and be part of the utopian idea. The biocosmist Aleksandr Svyatogor planned a 'house of immortality' that would abolish the dictatorship of time and space. He styled himself as a 'creator' and was infatuated by his great 'fighting community for the new age'.[8] 'It is time to prescribe another way for the Earth, he wrote. It would also be appropriate and the right moment to intervene in the orbit of other planets.'[9] Mastery of the Earth and the universe, the possibility of making history, interstellar human formats, bodies as projectiles to be shot into the beyond. Limits? Those without limits rule time and space.

The pull of the serpent's egg: as if something was growing under the veneer of time that made it difficult to understand in retrospect. It was already there but not yet born. It was already exerting its influence, although only in the mind. It could grow undisturbed, it could wait. It could do so much although it didn't yet exist. I looked at the words as they appeared successively on the display. Something was there. Something still without form, but already present.

Russia blazed through its revolutionary years. Dynamic, anarchic, fanatical, creative, heroic. Quiet spots? None. The old world was thrown into the melting pot of history and landed overnight by virtue of its birth in the gigantism of the modern Soviet world. It loved height and gravitated by being born around a Black Hole. It was called extinction. The more megalomaniacal the ideas, the more brutal the price in reality. This also applied to biocosmists, interplanetarianists and creators.

Svyatogor, author of the 'house of immortality', was arrested under Stalin's purging paranoia in June 1937 and sentenced to eight years in a camp. His fate was lost in nowhere land. Directly after the storming of the Winter Palace in St Petersburg, the biocosmist Aleksandr Yaroslavsky (1896–1930) called for the 'storming of the universe'. He was arrested in 1928 for 'defamation of the USSR in the foreign and white press', sentenced to five years in a camp and shot in 1930 on the Solovetsky Islands.[10]

Leon Trotsky, revolutionary from the earliest days and Stalin's great adversary, belongs to this phalanx as well. He was a bioutopianist and also wanted a complete shake-up. For him too it was a time of 'radical revision – of nature and mankind'.[11] 'Life, even pure physiological life, will become a collective experiment.'[12] Trotsky's beauty ideal? 'To create a higher sociobiological type, an übermensch, if you like.'[13]

The radiating bodies, the interplanetary travel, the people's palaces, the übermensch in the Bolshevist collective experiment. Psychology, biology, education, medicine, physiology, military research. Each and every one was to be the most modern, the newest, the best. Laboratory empires sprouted up from nowhere, immense amounts of public funding were made available, armies of researchers were recruited, the most contradictory and hare-brained ideas pursued. What appeared initially like openness often enough disintegrated as if overnight in the developing vortex of power.

Soviet bioutopias and their key metaphors: immortality, interplanetarianism, the New Man and his organ projections. As if the imagination were in the process of rewriting reality. Stalin demanded that research be confined to aspects that were practical and really of use to the New Man, who would modify and purge himself and be a missionary in his own interests. Someone who could reinvent himself through willpower, technology, breeding and Soviet education. And who was so new that it would also be possible for him to outrun his own genes. That, at least, was the plan.

'Brain equals head equals party.' This was the well-known formula of the first Russian Nobel Prize winner and conditioned reflex researcher Ivan Pavlov (1849–1936). The research cult of the brain was intended not only to solve the Lenin puzzle but also to explain the ingeniousness of the Soviet collective idea in principle. 'Proletarian biology' therefore designed breeding utopias, which placed life under the influence of the cerebral cortex. An attack above all on everything spontaneous, open, creative. A programme with long-term impact that also gave birth to creepily deformed research. Much of it was never allowed to be made public. Some of it was.

Hybrid. In 1926, the Soviet government decided to send an expedition with its star biologists to Kindia in French Guinea. As part of the ongoing hybridization research, they wanted to use human sperm to inseminate female chimpanzees at the chimpanzee station that had been set up there. A year later three females had already been inseminated, which led to 'a clear conclusion as far as the research was concerned'.[14] The researchers wanted more and developed the idea of inseminating 'African women with chimpanzee sperm'.[15] Both the governor of Guinea and the treating doctor at the hospital in Konakry refused to approve this bizarre experiment, and the Soviet biology team was forced to return home, albeit with a few chimpanzees in their baggage. These animals from Africa were part of the first experimental animals at a breeding farm in Sukhumi, Georgia.

I was reminded again of the tables where what we later called history was negotiated, the participants, the agendas, the seating arrangements. Of the Crimean sparkling wine at the beginning and end. Or was it vodka? Of the words that did not appear in any of the minutes. Of the looks and codes exchanged in an attempt to fit in. It's not as if it's too difficult to imagine. But there is always something left over that won't, that cannot and that refuses to be transmitted.

The New Man, young, clever, strong, powerful and energetic. It was a question of breeding, evolution, higher planes, the 'new Soviet man' and the scientific basis for a 'generally applicable procedure'.[16] It was also about the researchers in Sukhumi, who believed that they could 'very quickly modify the country's gene pool in accordance with a unified scientific plan'.[17] There was also the idea of the New Woman. 'In keeping with the general climate of the era, the women concerned were called upon to submit themselves to the experimental discipline. For participation in the crossbreeding experiments, it would be useful to identify at least five women to live for a year or more in strict isolation on the monkey breeding farm in Sukhumi.'[18] They should be interested theoretically but not materially in the experiments.[19]

Practical preparations were made, the experiments were started, but then in summer 1929, Tarzan, the only sexually mature anthropoid male on the Sukhumi farm, unexpectedly died. The research was suspended and a new group of monkeys acquired. In 1930 the leader of the research group was arrested and banished to Alma Ata, where he died in 1932. The obsessive research was put on ice. The experiments and records were buried by order in the Soviet archives until 1989.

Stalinist sciences. Almost a century has elapsed since then. What happened next? What became of all the early bioutopias after the Second World War? What of the heroism and presumption of the early days? And where did the Soviet and East German researchers pick up again after 1945? When did the secret research complexes begin to mesh?

The victory over Nazism had given the Soviet scientific elite a boost. They smelled fresh air. Hitler had been defeated, not least with the aid of strong Soviet military research. But there was still the same Stalin and the same ideological skirmishing. Genuine pauses for breath, more independent research? They existed, but only for a short time, only here and there, and only in opaque processes. 'It is no coincidence that the phases of particularly serious ideological interference in the late 1940s were connected with great privileges for scientists,' writes the historian Kirill Rossyanov.[20]

In the years of the Great Patriotic War, the New Man became the *Stalin Man*, defined as a radical absolute avant-gardist who was willing 'to give his entire life to new unknown forms,' as the philosopher Boris Groys put it.[21] In this furore, Stalin managed increasingly to align his policies with the research discourse in the country. He approved, promoted and paid above all anyone who was useful to his power and legacy. To that extent, it is logical that 'one of the last ideological embodiments of Stalinism focused in particular on the question of controlling heredity, in other words the extent to which the imprint of society can be transferred directly and systematically to the genetic material of plants, animals and humans. This did not weaken but rather gave additional strength to all earlier biologisms,' writes Gerd Koenen.[22]

Stalin died in March 1953. His empire had lasted thirty long years. When Nikita Khrushchev spoke in 1956 of the personal Stalin cult, he toppled Stalin from his übermensch throne.

It was followed by what was called the thaw, during which much was described as new and different, not least in the world of science. In retrospect it is clear how little was new in this new phase. This also applied to the GDR, Stalin's satellite state.

Can the factors influencing the systematic spread of viruses be determined and reproduced on Earth with a view to obtaining virus-free tissue?

Phytopathology proposals: experiments on breaking the propagation resistance of viruses; investigation of the influence of systemic propagation of viruses; investigation of possible changes – particularly genetically fixed mutations – in phytopathological viruses. Proposals for participation of the GDR Academy of Agricultural Sciences in the Interkosmos programme in the field of life sciences and agriculture, VD AL 00/7-5/79, Zentrales Archiv des Deutschen Zentrums für Luft- und Raumfahrt e.V., Göttingen, BAAR, A854, unnumbered.

Cybernetic lanterns

Dresden, childhood, Weisser Hirsch. From home, a hundred steps down to the Zwanziger, on the other side not quite as many up to the Rondell. Up on the left Villa San Remo, then Luisenhof, on the right the cable railway. On the Plattleite the huge Gründerzeit villas. In one of them was Hanna, and next door Steffen, both of them already waiting. On the balconies hollyhocks and cress, in the gardens white transparent apples and winter-flowering cherries. Clambering with these items through the net of childhood, with flakes of beauty and light. Along the Plattleite to the high, light-coloured wall. Behind the wall is the realm of Ardenne, well-guarded and accessible, of course, only for insiders. The sole exception: the gleaming copper observatory. And that's where we're going. It was Hanna, who kept on telling us in the morning at school that we could come in the evening to look at the sky. Hanna knew that. She was the daughter of the Ardenne technical director.

Hanna, Steffen, Suse, Hans, Peter and Petra, the gang. The simulated night sky, the magnificent telescope in the centre of the observatory, the slowly opening window to the cosmos. Our stellar evenings. And above all, the one and only Manfred von Ardenne, the unassailable Red Baron of our childhood.

Does he have a colour TV? How do you acquire an amazing villa like that? How long was he with the Russians, and could he be a KGB man? His aura pervaded the Weisser Hirsch, an aura of glamour, nobility and mystery. He was the exotic figure of my childhood, a kind of Dresden fata morgana. But who was he really?

He was born in Hamburg in 1907, a member of a prominent military family and of the 'white years', as they were called, those who were too young for military service before 1918 and too old by 1939. He submitted his first patent at the age of sixteen, the first of almost six hundred. He worked for himself from the age of seventeen and built telescopes, cameras and alarm systems. At the age of twenty-one he opened a private electron physics research institute in Berlin. He was fascinated by wireless moving images. He had drive and above all charisma. A youngster who grasped the dynamics of his time and crafted his own research style. His private Berlin laboratory remained in operation during the Nazi period. More than that, in 1942 he submitted a secret dossier that apparently served as a prototype for the purported "Hitler bomb" – the atom bomb – constructed at a weapons base in Bad Saarow.

After the war, he offered the Americans his knowledge and service.[1] The earlier arrival of the Red Army in Berlin thwarted this intention, and he was one of almost 3,000 German scientists forcibly taken to the Soviet Union as intellectual reparation.[2] The USA had dropped two atom bombs on Japan. Stalin needed one at all costs as well. In April 1945, Manfred von Ardenne, with his family and research institute, were taken by a special unit of the Red Army to a protected secret complex in Sinop, a suburb of Sukhumi. He was tasked with developing an isotope separation process. He succeeded. His research served as a basis for the detonation of the first Soviet hydrogen bomb in the Kazakh steppe in 1953. That same year, he was awarded the Stalin Prize, the Communist equivalent of the Nobel Prize, for his work.

Action men. He returned to Germany barely two years later. Almost fifty years old, he had spent ten years in the Soviet Union. How did he feel in Dresden, on the Weisser Hirsch, in his fairy-tale villa on the banks of the Elbe, below him a city in ruins? There are many possibilities. It's not as if he didn't write about it himself. But his texts read more like a cover-up than a personal confession of faith. His carefully prepared return to Germany was supervised by Walter Ulbricht, the new dictator in the East. He protected him and was his patron, enabling and consulting with him: 'Walter Ulbricht was a man of action who quickly recognized the essentials, listened attentively to his interlocutor's arguments and then swiftly came to a decision. For that reason, I regularly offered recommendations to him about what I considered to be necessary measures, changes or conclusions,' he wrote in his memoirs.[3]

1955. A time of blocs, reconstruction, pan-German trauma-induced delirium. The 1950s in the East. The hope, the reconstruction, the terror, the prohibitions, the political skirmishing, the shootings in Moscow. The early GDR and its quote 'innocence' unquote. The better, more peaceful Germany had one purpose: to press forward. There was no past. And the reality? Did the returnee from the Soviet Union in the Weisser Hirsch realize any of this? In the same year, he opened his private research institute for electron ion and nuclear physics on the picturesque banks of the Elbe. Although a member of the aristocracy and a private entrepreneur, he was a unique figure, who can still be seen as a prototype for the early research landscape of the East.

It was about project funding, access to the corridors of power, key positions and networking. About something that was to be reserved in particular for the Soviet returnees. Moscow had had good experiences with them. They could be trusted, at least a little. The authorities in East Berlin sought their favour and patronized them generously. An exclusive strategy that yielded success. Only a quarter of them settled in West Germany. The sciences thus mirrored what had long been the case in the political arena: not a step without the Kremlin's approval.

This power strategy is also reflected in many other biographies. The physicist and Nobel Prize winner Gustav Hertz (1887–1975) was seconded like Ardenne to Sukhumi in April 1945 and remained there nine long years to edge the Soviet atom bomb project towards success. He was also awarded the Stalin Prize for his research. After his return in 1955 he was appointed head of the Scientific Council for the Peaceful Use of Atomic Energy in the GDR Council of Ministers.

The poison gas expert Peter Adolf Thiessen (1899–1990), who had been expelled from the Prussian Academy of Sciences in 1945 because of his Nazi background, was also sent to Sukhumi with Ardenne and was also awarded the Stalin Prize. In 1957 he became chairperson of the newly established Research Council of the GDR, a coordinating link between the scientific, political and business sectors.

For no reason, after 1945 this trio was dubbed the 'Ardenne-Thiessen-Hertz protective ring'.[4] The need for lines of defence to ensure survival in the treacherous early days of the GDR runs like a leitmotif through the source material from these years. Jostling for position, jealousy of the experience of others, guilt dynamics, vicious attacks. The Ministry of State Security was founded in 1950. The next state within a state. The dense undergrowth of the post-war years thus became even more impenetrable and hazardous. Quite a few remained tangled in it.

Heinz Barwich (1911–66), born in Berlin, studied with Max Planck, Albert Einstein and Werner Heisenberg, obtained his doctorate in 1936 with Gustav Hertz and joined him in Siemens research laboratory II. After the war he was one of the few to go voluntarily to the Soviet Union, where he spent ten years. Directly after his return to East Germany, he was also entrusted with important positions, as adviser to the German

Academy of Sciences and first director of the Central Institute of Nuclear Research in Dresden-Rossendorf. In 1964 he fled to the West during the third International Conference on the Peaceful Uses of Nuclear Energy in Geneva. He said that the building of the Wall had been the final straw. He died two years later at the age of fifty-five.[5]

No questions. How unreal these biographies are. Not because they're incorrect, but because they weren't allowed to be made public. Nothing about the dazzling innovations of the Weimar Republic, nothing about the Hitler years, nothing about the Soviet years, nothing about what happened after the return in 1955 to what was now the German Democratic Republic. No breaks, no messing with history, no self-doubt. They were the bourgeois citizens, the old ones, immaculate and unrecognizable, transformed into monuments, symbolic beings, who were not questioned because they were untouchable. How was this historical window dressing and distance maintained so perfectly and for so long?

When the star scientists returned to the GDR from the Soviet Union in the mid-1950s, they were in effect beginners in a society that even ten years after the war was still struggling to find stability and some kind of normality. It had neither, just people observing, scrutinizing and denouncing one another. How was all that to be dealt with? Manfred von Ardenne did not look as if he intended to be held up unnecessarily by any entanglements. He started from the top with 'proposals for improving the utility of our research and development funding'.[6] He sent them directly to prime minister Otto Grotewohl. He demanded clarity, structure, concentration and the highest international standards. Industrial research should take place in the factories. There was also a need for a coordinating research committee. All this mess didn't make sense.

Ardenne quickly achieved his aims with regard to the new research institute, no doubt also because his proposal was in line with Ulbricht's policies. The Research Council of the GDR was founded in summer 1957 and became the pathway to key positions in practical research. Ardenne demanded just under 10 million marks for start-up investments.[7] A clear provocation. He knew it. He also knew that he would get his way. His demand was met secretly, by the highest authority in the country, Ulbricht himself. Details that say something about the climate in the early GDR years, about the clientelism in the new workers' and peasants' state, about the deals by the elites and the efforts by the new authorities to keep hold as far as possible of the pre-war intellectual giants. They were still needed.

Ardenne didn't take strolls around the Weisser Hirsch, stand in line at the grocer's for some food item that was in short supply or ride down to Körnerplatz on the cable railway. In normal life he was almost non-existent. Instead, he appeared regularly on television as the *éminence grise* whenever the parliament, the People's Chamber, met. The cameras focused on this lonely-looking man. He didn't seem special in any way. What was going through his mind? I can only recall this static image of him, which became strangely darker over the years.

Great pressures. The word cybernetics came originally from the military research conducted in the USA during the Second World War with a view to developing a technology for predicting the path of enemy aircraft. Simulations? The research was proceeding in the right direction, but the required megacomputers did not yet exist. The fact remains that *cybernetics*, as it came to be called, evolved 'in a climate of military control of research and efforts to automate and computerize the military during and after the Second World War,' as Philipp Aumann explains in *Mode und Methode: Die Kybernetik in der Bundesrepublik Deutschland.*[8] 'You have to anticipate, you have to include the movements of your potential target in your own calculations, you must operate in and address a future space,' added the philosopher Stefan Rieger in his take on the cybernetic phenomenon.[9]

Operating and addressing this future space was clearly what the global post-war world hungered after. No past any more, no world war disasters, no napalm wars, none of the environmental disasters that already existed at the time. The new truth was called the future, the stories took place in the future in the imaginary world of its users, in a space full of promise. Cybernetics moved naturally from the military field to civilian research and became a hyper-complex fear-management machine. At all events, it was a surrogate. It was styled as a social transmitter, a miracle drug, a modernization programme, a new language capable of completely transforming reality through pure and ecstatic technology. Cybernetics was hype, a superstar, a meta-phenomenon of a kind, to arm the new world against all possible fears, since the new technology could be planned, designed, automated and linked.

Wind. As might be imagined, the East had difficulties with the new-fangled wind, not least as it blew in from the USA. It rejected it. More than that, it opposed it. It was only after Stalin's death, after the Soviets had caught the world by surprise in 1957 with their Sputnik, after Georg Klaus, the foster father of East German cybernetics, in his book *Die Kybernetik in philosophischer Sicht* published in 1961, found the trick that reconciled party, state and economy as learning systems, that the resistance crumbled. The cyber-stars finally found favour, and soon there was no stopping them.[10] In physics, industry, psychology, design, architecture, the social sciences, art – from then on, those who bandied about buzzwords like 'scientific and technical progress' or 'cybernetics' were welcome as prime examples of how unstoppable Communism had become.

I think back to our visits as children to the observatory. What did we Wall children know about cybernetics in the 1960s? The word bobs around in my head like a lantern. Something that was meant to make things easier, brighter, better, that sounded somehow feasible and optimistic. Was that it? Punched cards, control units, laboratories, machine rooms. We painted highways to the sky, redirected the Elbe to enable huge dams to be built, designed new multilevel cities. My childhood memory must have been a high-rise building.

I managed to acquire possibly the last copy of the GDR year 11 physics textbook from Amazon.[11] It arrived the next day, seventh edition, 1969. The text promised an introduction to cybernetics. On page 74, the trusty Yuri Gagarin was orbiting the Earth in his spaceship *Vostok*. 12 April 1961. I wasn't yet one year old. The Berlin Wall would be built four months later.

Next to Gagarin's spherical rocket the sentence: 'Designing rocket engines calls for precise knowledge of the behaviour of bodies at high temperatures and under great pressure.'[12] In the chapter 'Mechanics': 'Kinetic energy exists when a body is put in motion through acceleration.'[13] I think of Manfred von Ardenne, cybernetics and my childhood. Of apparatus, capsules and something very narrow, the eye of a needle that we had first to go through it seems, to be hurled into our flight path.

Recalls. In the early 1960s the GDR was in a hopeless crisis. A rapidly growing number of refugees were fleeing to the West. Doctors, engineers and artists in particular were turning their back on the country. The economy was failing. The conclusion of the forced collectivization of agriculture in April 1960 had taken its toll. Unpredictability, pressure and shortages dominated everyday life. Then on 13 August 1961 the building of the Berlin Wall, which, after the founding of the state in 1949 and the repression of the popular uprising on 17 June 1953, was seen as the third 'internal founding of the GDR'.[14]

People wanted to have the strength to start over, to leave the ruins behind them and to see the great vision take wing. Cybernetics appeared as the long sought-after and above all practical vehicle for this project of hope. It was there and sounded chic, it had something international about it, and it was sexy. All this promised the possibility of moving on from the critical early years in the East, the terror of the Stalin era, and would perhaps enable people to forget the fact of being politically corseted. A surplus of utopia through research and technology, and thus more stable, progressive times.

A cybernetics department was established in the Academy of Sciences in 1962, cybernetics departments sprang up in universities, and cybernetics suddenly became part of the school curriculum. In 1963, Ulbricht approved the New Economic System, which focused on reform, pragmatism and economic efficiency. Cybernetics was ideal here too for promoting this strategy. Through it some kind of common denominator could be found for even the most disparate practical problems.

Through cybernetics, the GDR entered the modern world on its own terms. But the New Economic System and the East German cyber-mania were both short-lived. Too much openness, too much structural dynamics. In October 1964, Khrushchev, who had vanquished Stalinism, was removed from office in a coup-like move. His demise marked the end of the promised reforms, not only in the Soviet Union but also in the GDR. In early December 1965, Erich Apel, head of the State Planning Commission and the driving force behind the East German economic reforms, shot himself in his Berlin office in the House of Ministries. His system of economic self-determination that had sought to assert itself in the face of all opposition was thus without a head.

Ultimately, it was SED chief ideologist Kurt Hager who put an end to the dalliance with cybernetics directly after the Prague Spring. The supreme discipline had proved to be too much competition for the central Marxist programme. End, finished, over. After 1968 another general overhaul and exploratory programmes. Cybernetics was no longer worshipped, even though it was occasionally consulted in secret military dossiers or conspiratorial state planning tasks and even though a Central Institute for Cybernetics and Information Processing still worked quietly in the background. But by the early 1970s the role of cybernetics as a social transmitter was over.

The experience of moon landings shows, however, that man can quickly adapt his manner of walking and the entire musculoskeletal apparatus to the conditions of reduced gravitation. A wide-legged, jump-like stride appears to be the most effective way of moving.

Haase, 'Tauglichkeit', BArch, DVW 2-1/39885, p. 116, unnumbered.

No admission for unauthorized persons

Secure zones. I spent summer 2018 in the archive in Freiburg. No sign of the military-industrial complex. It was not mentioned in any dossier. Nothing about the unknown soldier either. No sweetie e-mails. Radio silence. But that didn't necessarily prove anything. Does something not exist just because there is no mention of it? My task that summer was thus one of extensive reconnaissance: minutes of faculty meetings, formerly secret doctoral theses, research concepts, executive orders, academic conferences. I pored over the scant documents and thought, OK, it's not going anywhere at the moment, but just sit tight. There is something. I don't know what, but it will reveal itself.

The New Man, with a body that was no longer organ-based. Was he a project that was shot into the future to be played with? An early cyborg? What would later be called the 'Interkosmos programme' is recorded as having started on 13 April 1967. Specialists from nine countries in the Soviet orbit met in Moscow at the end of a cold April week to launch the ultimate research complex: the exploration and use of space.[1]

It looked like something of fundamental significance, something the GDR had in fact approved two years previously. It was no doubt important as well because space research in the post-war East German academic landscape had not been particularly prominent. Too historically encumbered, too expensive, not politically feasible. Was a relaunch now conceivable under Soviet patronage, twenty years after the end of the Nazi period? The East German population as a whole initially knew nothing of what was going on in Moscow. The whole thing was top secret. That's what the secret services were for. The GDR secret police immediately sealed the restricted areas concerned as being critical to operations and turned them into secure military complexes. The Moscow Agreements of 1967 were based 'essentially on secret and top secret technology and documentation'.[2] Stasi head Erich Mielke issued Order 2/67 to that effect. It contained detailed instructions as to how the research was to be passed off as a state secret: mandatory meetings, top-level confidentiality, secret security and research concepts, a Stasi network in key positions, master card files, operation plans, detailed information reports, designation of key personnel, enemy intelligence.[3] Research with different confidentiality classifications, depending on its relevance: secret, confidential, classified, restricted, official.*

The top GDR research programmes were protected as a cluster system in which outside the secret service a dozen people at most, usually fewer, were given 'general information' about the project in question. The carefully selected persons had to sign confidentiality agreements: 'I undertake to keep in strict confidence all facts, objects or information I become aware of in connection with the Interkosmos programme, in particular information about proposals for scientific experiments other than those submitted by my facility. I have been informed of the disciplinary or criminal consequences of violations of this undertaking.'[4] The actual punishments were also

---

* Geheime Kommandosache, Geheime Verschlusssache, Vertrauliche Verschlusssache, Vertrauliche Dienstsache, Nur für den Dienstgebrauch.

indicated. According to the Criminal Code they were severe: at least five years' imprisonment for espionage, up to twelve years for treasonable communication of information, up to five years for unauthorized disclosure of research.[5]

Research departments were transformed accordingly into security zones and 'hidden from the outside'.[6] Thus no one could enter the inner enclaves of this high-level scientific research without authorization. No unauthorized persons, no disclosed information, nothing unchecked. Within the conspiratorial research zone, the 'formation of a solid commitment to confidentiality' was demanded.[7] As if people, buildings, sites could be wrapped in electrified fencing. Is it possible to order such a thing? How can it be tolerated in the long term? And which people, which buildings, which sites?

Equilibrium. Material with many doors, many corridors and annexes, much underflooring, much hinterland. Barely has the material appeared than it is transformed into a dynamic system. The words come with difficulty, are slow in forming, some don't want at first to be part of it. What words can be used? I leaf through the files. A government decision of 1955 states that GDR military doctors are to be trained exclusively in Greifswald. The project meanders. There was a lack of manpower, logistics, structure. Progress was slow. In 1963 the decision to outsource military medical training to the Ernst-Moritz-Arndt University of Greifswald. In 1970 the Faculty of Military Medicine was established and authorized to award academic degrees.

From the minutes of the faculty meeting of the Military Medicine section of March 1971: 'The dean explained the need to find teaching staff for military medicine.'[8] Eighteen months later: 'Question on the requirements for the new chairs for military and military medicine disciplines at the universities of Rostock, Leipzig and Berlin. Close collaboration with the Russians.'[9] In the meantime, new and serious platforms were also being built at another level. The Interkosmos programme had taken off as a result of internal discussions between the authorities and the scientific community. But who made the decisions? Who met? Where? What did they discuss?

In front of me on the table in Freiburg is May 1975. Doctoral degrees are awarded at the university in Greifswald, military medicine section. The guest speaker talks about 'the experience of Soviet military medicine', about 'chemical warfare agents and biological weapons of mass destruction', about 'research results on human equilibrium', about 'diode technology and cybernetics', about 'higher levels of combat readiness', about 'overcoming organ-based thinking and the development of human-environment systems, a condition for conquering extraterrestrial space'.[10]

There he is again, the New Body. I try to imagine what it all means exactly: mastery of organ-based thinking. Human-environment systems. Conquering extraterrestrial space. The words make me dizzy. They are too powerful, too dense, too compact. Of course, I understand, this is the military. It's about domination and conquest. And yet to all appearances it would seem that the words themselves must first of all recognize what they are saying.

Total research. The sky as an expression of will, also as the symbol of a desire for change. The cybernetic revolution with its key metaphors, which in retrospect were not so new: limitless potential, belief in engineering, 'the all-defining technology', the obsession with efficiency.[11] The enthusiasm at the time must have been real. I go back. In the Greifswald minutes of 1971, the phrase: 'Close collaboration with the Russians'. Where did that come from?

The body 'under extreme conditions' had a history in Soviet military research.[12] It combined the powerful bioutopian schools of the old Russia with the post-revolution schools and later also the Stalin era. A biomedical research complex was founded in Leningrad in the 1930s for the 'total investigation of man', comparable to 'gigantic industry projects such as the Dnieper dams and the Magnitogorsk iron and steel works'.[13] One of the most prominent figures in Soviet extreme research was the physiologist and Pavlov student Leon Orbeli (1882–1958), whose work formed the basis for Soviet space medicine. Orbeli spoke of the 'occupation of the stratosphere as a transition to completely new living conditions'.[14] During the Second World War he was head of air force medicine and tested the Russian versions of amphetamines and Pervitin on tank drivers and pilots[15] – substances for staying awake that were 'ideal companions on the battlefield', that could keep troops going if necessary for three days and nights.[16] Pervitin, the war drug that also lowered inhibitions. The problem with it was that it was highly addictive, so much so that the historian wrote of a 'tendency to act in an artificial delusional world'.[17]

The Stalin era with the formulated aim of finding 'a generally practicable process' for breeding the New Man.[18] And the dictator himself, who sought to 'have control over all aspects of social life'.[19] An idea that was to be transferred to space like an ideological law of nature. The aim was not just total control but also being the first to make it possible to live for long periods in space. Communism as world revolution transferrable to the universe.

Droplets and thorn apple. Back to Hans Haase's cosmonaut study, which features the New Body as a kind of blueprint. He said of weightlessness: 'The blood is redistributed from the bottom up. Consequence: increased amount of blood in the organs of the thorax and head. Increase by 39 to 46 per cent in relative pulse volume in the head, the eyes and the chest, difficulty in nasal breathing, sensation similar to the start of influenza. The face is bloated, the folds in the skin disappear, the tissues above the heart become oedematous.'[20]

Oedematous, anaemic, haematological, atrophic. If the body of the future does not regress, it will shrink and in this way become the weakest combatant in the stellar conquest project. It is the most vulnerable and exposed part of the project. Put another way, the old body cannot survive in the new sky. It's in the way. The extent of the bodily implosion was known at the latest with Pavlov and his disciple Leon Orbeli, since the Soviet military research during the Second World War. The limits had been set. That should have brought people to their senses. The opposite occurred. The longing for the New Man continued. The response to the rejection by space was a rigorous 'conjuncture of the military'.[21] Focus: specialized major research.

The first Soviet cosmonaut group was selected in early 1960 from a pool of 3,000 pilots. Four hundred made it to the second round. At the end there were twenty remaining, including Yuri Gagarin, the first man in space. Almost all of them belonged to the war children generation and were in their mid-twenties when they were stylized as national heroes. They were required to wave, hold flags, smile – and die. Often at a very young age, of cancer, heart failure, alcohol or accidents. Today we would describe them as classic victims of chemical substances.

Regarding this problem, Haase noted in his study that the cosmonaut would lose 'around 20 per cent of his leg strength and about 10 per cent of his arm strength during the first four weeks of flight'. His conclusion: 'In the author's opinion, anabolic steroids could help to prevent the development of muscular atrophy. For longer missions, the administration of this substance should be combined with regular physical training and a special diet.'[22]

According to him, there was thus a solution for muscular atrophy. But what about the bones, the blood and the organs? In keeping with the times, the Haase study pays very close attention to the blood. For both short and longer space flights, it says, there are 'characteristic changes in the haematological parameters',[23] particularly during long flights. The crews who spent between 96 and 175 days in the Salyut-6 space station lost up to 24 per cent of their haemoglobin.[24] This in turn led to 'up to 25 per cent loss of bone substance and disruption of the bone metabolism'.[25]

And there was more. The researchers observed marked changes in the erythrocytes, the red blood cells, in weightless conditions. Some of the long-term crews 'were found on their return to Earth with erythrocytes in the shape of thorn-apples, bells, ellipses and droplets. The profusion of these relatively old erythrocyte forms was accompanied by a reduction in newer forms.'[26] Further research was essential, it went on, to 'exclude a pathological mechanism'.[27]

From the early stages of space travel, some Soviet cosmonauts reported a subjectively changed hearing capability under the influence of weightlessness. They stated that all noises were perceived as louder and higher-pitched. One possible explanation is that the weightlessness of the ossicles causes changes in the sound conduction impedance, particularly at high frequencies. Another explanation is that the redistribution of the blood in the organism causes changes in sound volume perception in the head. A third theory is that the absence of spatial orientation because of the weightless state of the vestibular apparatus causes disruptions in neural information processing.

Zentrales Archiv des Deutschen Zentrums für Luft- und Raumfahrt e.V., Göttingen, BAAR, A8 47, unnumbered.

Weightlessness

Deeper lying. Why did we have a notion of something like the military-industrial complex while studying in Jena? Where did the term come from? Who talked about it? Why was it such a familiar concept for us?

It was 17 January 1961, when US President Dwight D. Eisenhower ended his period of office with a remarkable farewell address: 'In the councils of government, we must guard against the acquisition of unwarranted influence, whether sought or unsought, by the military-industrial complex. The potential for the disastrous rise of misplaced power exists and will persist. We must never let the weight of this combination endanger our liberties or democratic processes. We should take nothing for granted.'[1]

The speech is available on YouTube. The seriousness with which the outgoing US President addressed the population is particularly striking. Eisenhower apparently saw sufficient evidence that illegitimate power systems outside parliament were in operation and regarded what in his eyes had already been going on for years as a fundamental attack on the United States of America. He provided no proof that a military-industrial complex existed. There was probably no need. His farewell address was meant above all as a warning and appeal and also an attempt to make this intangible power more tangible. In his address, the outgoing president did not question the complete inviolability that was clearly written into the DNA of the United States. He was alarmed at the way this inviolability had for some time been used in a way that jeopardized the state. He was referring to old and newly forming networks, to often bizarre and uninhibited careers, to deliberate obfuscation. The military-industrial complex as a hybrid shadow system that sought to legitimize itself above all by defending the idea of America as a superpower.

The historian Holger H. Herwig traces this self-proclaimed inner bulwark back to colonial times. He describes the power network operating covertly in the USA that had developed enormously in the First and Second World War and had become even more ramified under the new conditions of the Cold War.[2] This military big business also often involved German Nazi researchers bought by the Allies after 1945 to exploit Hitler's terrible expertise. The protagonists carrying out nuclear weapons research are well known, those investigating biological warfare less so.

Of the many scientists brought to the USA after 1945, two stand out. The doctor Walter Paul Schreiber (1893–1970) was head physician at the 1936 Olympic Games in Berlin and professor at the Military Medicine Academy in 1943. After being appointed to the Reich Research Council, he was a member of Hitler's internal research team responsible for countless human experiments in German concentration camps, including the mescaline studies in Dachau. From then on, Schreiber became the specialist in drugs and torture.[3] In 1945 the Soviets interned him in a penal camp near Moscow and pressured him to testify in the Nuremberg Trials. After his release from Soviet captivity, he became a doctor in the East German Volkspolizei.

Schreiber fled in 1948 to West Berlin, and the Americans moved him to the Counter Intelligence Corps (CIC) in

Oberursel. The US Army interrogation centre wanted to exploit his experience in the use of special interrogation techniques, including the administration of mescaline, to get defectors and prisoners to talk. In 1951 he moved to the notorious Randolph Air Force Base in Texas in connection with Operation Paperclip. His work there, together with Professor Hubertus Strughold, also a Dachau doctor: 'Survival training experiments on troops in isolated regions of the world'.[4] Forced under public pressure to leave the USA in 1951, he died in Argentina in 1970.

The doctor Kurt Blome (1894–1969), a racist, antisemite and early member of the Nazi Party, rose rapidly during the Nazi period under the protection of Heinrich Himmler and became the central figure in the Wehrmacht for biological warfare. He was Sanitätsgruppenführer in the SA, deputy Reichsärzteführer, honorary professor in the Faculty of Medicine in Berlin, and member of the Reich Research Council, where he was responsible for 'Rassenpflege' (racial purity) and later for 'cancer research,' according to the medical historian Ernst Klee the 'cover name for biological weapons'.[5] Despite incontestable proof of his virus and bacteria experiments using human subjects in a number of concentration camps and the hugely incriminating evidence by Walter Paul Schreiber in court, he was acquitted in the Nuremberg Doctors' Trial. After his rehabilitation, Blome was released from prison in 1947. Was it a tactic or a deal to recruit someone like him surreptitiously for biological weapon research in the USA?

Blome at least knew how to sell himself to the Americans. His statements were evidently heard, no doubt also because the USA at the time anticipated that the Soviets would be the first to use biological weapons through 'sabotage attacks with botulinum toxin or a worldwide pneumonic plague epidemic' with 'deadly germs or poisons'. Blome was therefore recruited by the US Army as Walter Paul Schreiber's successor in the interrogation centre in Oberursel. His project: 'army 1952, project 1972'. The nature of this work has still not been made public today.

Improved animals. The military-industrial complex became a known concept at the latest through Eisenhower's address in 1961. It is a concept that automatically conjured up certain associations and, depending on political interests, was explained away, exaggerated or hushed up. It was useful for conspiracy theories, for the idea of the deep state, and as a cover for massive armaments deals. It was the Cold War. A war that was also used as an excuse for the rapidly growing military expenditure, for the blurring of the boundaries between the military and the civilian sectors, and for dividing the world between the two superpowers.

Already in 1958, at Eisenhower's initiative, an early form of the Defence Advanced Research Projects Agency (DARPA), was created as the official Pentagon think tank and a counter-strategy to the military-industrial complex. DARPA as a means of containing the military-industrial complex? As a space for possible futures, radical ideas, high risk and an explicit practical approach. Not by chance, DARPA's growing interest in physical and neural enhancement coincided with the development of genetic and genome research. Since the 1950s, the USA had made rapid progress in this research. The programme: optimization of the inner workings of the human body – the cells, genes, nerves and even the possibility of creating human life in the laboratory. Criticisms of legally questionable research interests were countered with pat responses that those who sought to limit the research were overly pessimistic or endangering freedom. There was thus this highly sensitive US research mission, characterized as well by an excess of pragmatism. This had historical reasons but resulted in an increasing shift in discussion from humans to the notion of what constituted a *person*. According to the bioethicist James Hughes, who invented the label 'cyborg citizenship', persons

were defined as 'all self-aware forms of life', in other words
'conventional' and transhuman people, hybrids, clones, intel-
ligent robots, 'improved' animals. 'Not all persons are humans,'
he claimed, 'and not all humans are persons.'

It is questionable whether Eisenhower's warning had an
impact in the USA in the 1960s. And what about the military-
industrial complex? Did it exist or not? The definitive proof
of its existence in the USA could not ultimately be provided.
According to Holger H. Herwig, the 'primary sources were too
limited' and 'documents in armament company safes are still
inaccessible'.[6] But the whole thing could not simply be ignored
as a quirk, cliché or dubious invention by the President.
Herwig points out that the deeper-lying arsenal of the military-
industrial complex subsequently grew extra limbs, with the
result that there are possibly at least five military complexes
today in the USA connected in particular with oil, Congress,
think tanks and the Church.[7]

Special subjects. I am standing in the Freiburg archive car
park smoking a cigarette. It's August 2018, September 2018,
early October 2018. It's still summer and no shade anywhere.
Have I made any progress? Has anything become clearer? The
material appears to be spreading its roots like a rhizome. I feel
like I'm all over the place in time. And again and again the time
after the war. Like the format for a never-ending story. As if
someone had determined the seating arrangement and laid out
the combat utensils.

This morning finally a file on the Institute for Aerospace
Medicine on a counter in the Königsbrück archive near
Dresden. An annual medical report from 1964/65.

'During the reporting period 761 patients were admitted to
hospital,' it says. 'Of these patients, 360 were special subjects.
Among the patients were 120 civilians and 179 conscripts.'
Then the addition: 'Exercise in the low-pressure chamber,
pressure chamber ascent, barometer function, EEG, hypoxia

ascent (5000 m), pressure chamber ascent for experimental purposes, acclimatization of amateur and top athletes.'[8]

I recall Jacob and our meeting in Berlin. How he stood there. How he showed the photos to me. How he wanted to know. As if he were asking from afar: So, what's it about? Was I also one of the special subjects? What does 'experimental purposes' mean? He didn't say anything about the low-pressure chambers, or about ascents and acclimatization. So it must have been about something else. But shouldn't I meet up with him again? Or should I carry on reading first? How much retro-activity can a life put up with? How many threads, how many theatres, how much invisibility? The GDR has been history for thirty years. On the street in Freiburg footsteps, cars, the endless summer as a shimmering silhouette. A Berlin number on my iPhone display. The Doping-Opfer-Hilfe advice centre. Hanna asks: Have you read it yet? – What? – The article in *Nordkurier*. – I'm in the archive and haven't heard anything. – Something terrible. Read it first. You're also mentioned.

Another day that I can't get out of my head. I know that I got through the archive checkpoint, felt the icy pneumatic suction, that it went click again, and that I opened my Mac laptop in the reading room. What had I imagined? Had I imagined anything at all? I searched on the Internet for *Nordkurier*, a Neubrandenburg regional newspaper. Let's see. Did I think that? Ropes, batons, arsenals. Do people really think that? Read it first, Hanna had said.

The article was simply an attack on the Doping-Opfer-Hilfe, on our work and on me. Accusations of dirty dealing, supposedly exaggerated figures. The victims were freeloaders and cry babies who needed to be exposed as liars. I was surprised, but then again not. In the previous years we had been politically active. We had opened an advice centre in Berlin, fought for compensation, initiated research and started cooperation. It was going too slowly, certainly, but the story could no longer be hushed up. A survey of the damage had been gradually established, related for the most part by the Wall generation. In 2018 our work appeared finally to be on the verge of institutionalization. And now this: a fierce attack on a political project and victim group. What was going on? What were we dealing with? What were we in for? Who were the protagonists? What was their motive?

Unknown soldier. I don't know why he sprang to mind again. Or when I started to ask if they were perhaps connected: the attempt to publicize the physical trauma of the East, to make it more visible, and the attempt to prevent precisely that. At all events, the figure in the mist was not in any hurry. The sentence with fine-tuning. That was five months ago. But why should the unknown soldier and a regional newspaper in north Germany have anything to do with one another? Where was the connection? It occurred to me merely that something was apparently going on here that had not yet been processed, not understood, not clearly identified. The *Nordkurier* attack hit the victims with full force. Our project began to wobble. Weightlessness. What was to be done? Perhaps carry on sitting in the archive for a while.

Sclerotic. Some 781 cadre companies and hence 'enterprises that almost exclusively manufactured arms, munition and military equipment', 270 research and development facilities, 3 million people.[9] That was the Soviet military-industrial complex in the 1950s. The Second World War was over but it signified not peace but total rearmament. Entire sections of the military sprouted from the ground, also thanks to the German research transfer. 'From 1947 to 1949 alone, Stalin's atomic bomb project cost more than 14.5 billion roubles.'[10]

It was not until 1961 – the year in which Eisenhower attempted to heighten Western awareness with his urgent military-industrial complex speech – that the Soviets had enough military bases, equipment, research and material to wage a nuclear war. In retrospect, the two are connected, particularly the fears of both sides. At the time, however, they operated with offensive strategies, with strict confidentiality, with acquisition programmes, decisive battlefields, long-range bomber fleets, operational aerial reconnaissance.

Every year the endless military parades past the Kremlin: a goose-stepping army, soldiers heroically thrusting their legs up above their heads, faces dissolving in block-formations. Behind them thousands of tonnes of steel rattling, rumbling and shining. Armies of weapons that were beginning to strangle the country. Stalin died and left behind his entrenched rearmament doctrine, non-negotiable either under Khrushchev or Brezhnev. Through it came the gradual formation of a sclerotic state.

Star Wars East. And the military-industrial complex in the GDR? Experts emphasize that a military-industrial complex can develop only where there is an arms industry, a project that the GDR had to finally put on ice with the building of the Wall in 1961. Was it possible to have a military-industrial complex without an arms industry? There are some grounds for not immediately dismissing this question out of hand and several reasons why the background to the military-industrial complex and the GDR is unclear. One is the general 'Soviet control of GDR armament'.[11] There was nothing in this area that could be decided or undertaken independently of the big brother country. The Soviet military-industrial complex thus extended over the years into the GDR, where it sought to develop in the shadows.

A further reason why the question of the military-industrial complex in the GDR cannot be simply explained is the close interconnection between civilian, military and secret service activities. How were they to be separated? Who did what within this network? For whom? With what designs? Why? Who signed the service contracts? Who secured them? Who paid? The fact alone that already in the 1970s, 30 per cent of production in the Carl Zeiss Jena group had to do with armaments is a clear example of what the historian Torsten Diedrich refers to as 'special production'.[12] 'There is no question that the rearmament and militarization of the GDR left deep traces in the finance system and the country's economy. They made an important contribution to the increase in the GDR's national debt to 123 billion GDR marks.'[13]

The third reason for the lack of clarity in the East German military-industrial complex phenomenon is the great secrecy and covering up. The clandestine cluster research, the special links by scientific and special institutions with the West and the separate contracts by GDR research facilities with the Soviet Union form a huge jigsaw puzzle. On the one hand, government planning tasks were centrally procured and monitored and required ministerial approval. On the other hand, an astonishing amount was possible when big or small dictators wanted to indulge their whims.

The fourth obstacle to explaining an East German military-industrial complex could well have been the GDR's emphatic fairy-tale dogma. However much research, however many arms, however large the army in the country, according to the official narrative they served solely to protect the homeland and to foster progress and peace. Even after 1989, this myth was able to survive, remain intact and even regenerate itself in the face of all sources that indicated a different story. The historian Reinhard Buthmann attempted to debunk this legend through his research, pointing to the predominance of military projects, particularly in the last decade of the GDR. Back in 1977 the Soviets had already proposed to the GDR 'the development of a system of automated orientation of spacecraft in the cosmos', as a result of which the government launched a 'complex armaments programme'.[14] With the agreement of GDR boss Erich Honecker to the Soviet programme to combat Ronald Reagan's Strategic Defensive Initiative (SDI) in 1983, 'the GDR finally abandoned its non-military space research,' says Buthmann.[15]

Would the GDR have imploded differently in 1989, or would it not have imploded at all at this time if it had not strangled itself like its Soviet guiding light through the rampant armaments mania? State-of-the-art weapons systems, key technologies, anti-SDI, massive security complexes. The technical military component of the Interkosmos research has now been largely confirmed, identified and narrated in the source material. But where is the New Man in Star Wars East?

The installation of a centrifuge on board was new in comparison to earlier biosatellites. . . . Twenty-five rats were taken on board in special bio-containers. Among the results obtained, it was reported that the test animals grew much less than the terrestrial control group.

Report on the ninth meeting of the scientific symposium of the Socialist States Standing Working Group on Cosmic Biology and Medicine (Cosmic Physiology Section), Königsbrück, 21 June 1976, Zentrales Archiv des Deutschen Zentrums für Luft- und Raumfahrt e.V., Göttingen, BAAR, A857, unnumbered.

Coupling manoeuvre

Naked. The first space mission with GDR participation was the satellite Interkosmos-1, which was launched into orbit on 14 October 1969. Until then, the East German institutes had been involved only in the technical ground programmes. The contribution to Interkosmos-1 was also of a purely technical nature: a UV photometer, a telemetry transmitter, a power supply unit.[1] But this launch was not purely symbolic, because from this date space research finally became a fixed component of the GDR planning strategies.[2] From then on there were 'government plans', 'separate budget items', 'central research projects', in other words lots of money. Research was ordered, institutes, commissions, working groups, new special units were formed. There were laboratories, new buildings, resources and careers. There were also widespread cooperation projects. A working report from 1973 stated: 'The Institute for Aerospace Medicine has cooperative relations with the institutes for aerospace medicine in Moscow, Prague and Warsaw. The Institute director describes the preservation and further development of this cooperation as vital and indispensable.'[3]

Restructuring, expansion, professionalization on all fronts. It was not a start from scratch but one that catapulted secret state space research into a new era, also in terms of biopolitics. At the same time, under the dictatorship the body was highly exposed. A battlefield and a parade ground. It was a place of power and hence also its visualization, demonstration and presentation. It was a place with a purpose, an external marking and an internal design. The body was 'naked fear'.[4] It was the interface between the individual and collective memory. And it became a conceptual platform in which power could also ultimately implode. The body thus became the starting point for self-empowerment, a last refuge of intimacy, self-defence.

What if there was not this one large, long table, at which the dictator body was defined? What if there were lots of smaller ones? Something here, someone there, different thoughts, people nodding and coming to all kinds of agreements. What if it was not quite as we had assumed? Then, I would also have to go to another archive. Then, what I was looking for would not be in Freiburg but possibly somewhere completely different. But where?

November 2018. Archive of the Academy of Sciences on Gendarmenmarkt in Berlin. The plans for bioscientific cosmic physics research from the year 1973. Although it was early days, they sound quite clear. 'Future biological research' should 'create the conditions for modifying genetic information, increasing mental and physical capabilities, controlling mental processes including learning and memory, and influencing ageing processes and pathological disorders.'[5] At this point the country changed from prognosis to long-term planning.[6] The system was looking to the future. The Academy of Sciences and industrial research had to connect to make good the growing deficits. This process was called 'Academy reform'. The keywords: innovative material, innovative appliances, innovative test procedures, innovative performance data. In 1971 the research association MOGEVUS – Molecular Basis for Development, Inheritance and Control Processes – was established. Looking back, it seems in fact to have focused mainly on developing new pharmaceuticals. Erich Honecker, the second dictator in the East with his nationalist tic, took over the rudder. The Academy of Sciences, whose fifty institutes had managed until then to appoint directors without party affiliation and which had recruited many researchers who were able to move between East and West Germany, was now restructured and in 1972 renamed Academy of Sciences of the GDR. The country was becoming increasingly interconnected. It was called 'the research drive'.

Towards the end of 1973, the Council of Ministers adopted a decision to 'expand the GDR contribution to the Interkosmos programme'.[7] A regulation with wide ramifications, because it also contained 'military aspects'.[8] In 1974 the GDR took part officially for the first time in the consultations of the Cosmic Biology and Medicine section in Bucharest.[9] The subjects discussed included weightlessness, illusion and deficiencies in spatial perception, radiation research, gas milieus, maximum acceleration loads, noise level, vibrations and the mental state of the cosmonauts.[10] According to the report by the participating aerospace medicine specialist Hans Haase from Königsbrück, the results were 'useful for cosmic biology and medicine, and for the various human medicine disciplines, including clinical medicine, industrial and sports medicine, and aerospace medicine and psychology'.[11] The head of the Permanent Cosmic Biology and Medicine Working Group was specially chosen in 1975.[12] And at the end of 1976 the Ministry of Science stated: 'To train our own cosmonauts, we will need to step up work on cosmic medicine and biology in the GDR.'[13]

It requires a special ability to observe history as if from the window of a train carriage. As if it were constantly passing by in the landscape. With many people in it – rebuilding, training, re-educating, getting down to work. A week before Christmas 1976, Sigmund Jähn and Eberhard Köllner were at the Yuri Gagarin training centre in Moscow. They had arrived only a few days earlier. What had they discovered since their arrival? Had they already been removed from the winter weather in Moscow and put in the 60-degree thermal chamber? Were they able to bring their families with them? At all events, Sigmund Jähn didn't yet know that he would be the first German in space. He also didn't know the programmes, procedures and projections that he would have to participate in to become a body representing the nation. He was to become the most thoroughly investigated body in the GDR.

We would like to see history as a pale landscape, disappearing, vanished. Like a shadow without a body. Still, held at bay. Suddenly, however, for some unknown reason, it comes back, reappearing out of the shadows into the present. As if it was returning in a second life. What would Sigmund Jähn's body tell us today?

Substitutes and drive. The Faculty of Military Medicine at the University of Greifswald set the research pace from the early 1970s onwards within the East German army. In 1971, 120 doctoral degrees were defended, in 1975 it was 312, and in 1980 no fewer than 827.[14] Many of the doctoral theses were incorporated directly in central military research projects.[15] The department was enlarged. The early projects essentially revolved around the stellar high-performance cosmonaut with his controlled implosions in weightless conditions. This focus was to remain. Substitutes were needed for blood, muscles, bones, damaged ears, eyes, heart, spleen, basically everything. It occurs to me that perhaps state secrets are also beings. They have advocates, are decided, exist at some point, go through germinating phases and then get going.

The four military research institutes in the country: the Greifswald Military Medicine section, the Königsbrück Institute for Aerospace Medicine, the Stralsund Navy Medicine Centre, and the Central Military Hospital and their research drive.[16]

The 'leading comrades of the party and state leadership' and their research drive.[17]

The Ministry for State Security and the Ministry of the Interior and their research drive.[18]

The specialists from the Academy of Sciences of the GDR and their research drive.

The specialist facilities and groups and their often idiosyncratic research drive: the Diagnostic and Consultancy Centre for Medical Genetics,[19] the Institute for Material Research in Berlin, the Ardennes Research Institute for Electron Ion and Nuclear Physics, the Research Institute for Medical Diagnosis, the VEB Pharmaceutical Group GERMED in Dresden, to name but a few.

Coordination of military medical scientific research with the Königsbrück Institute for Aerospace Medicine, the Academy of Sciences, the fraternal armies, the Ministry of Health[20] and the resultant research drive.

The consultation programmes, among others, with the Academy of Military Medicine of the Kirov Academy in Leningrad[21] and the interlinked research drive.

The research from 1977 between the 'Charité specialists' and 'Soviet specialists from the IMBP as part of the Interkosmos programme'[22] and their fast-tracked research drive.

The Institute for Medical Biological Problems (IMBP) was the leading authority in the Ministry of Health of the Soviet Union, which from 1973 regularly launched 'biosputniks' as part of the BION project, a satellite programme to investigate biological processes in space. 'The collaboration can be described as professional, reciprocal, effective and friendly. High points of this collaboration were the Kosmos 1129 and Kosmos 1514 biosatellite experiments.'[23]

There was, of course, more to the research drive. But I have to take a break, go for a walk, let it all sink in. It's already November, but the days have a pre-spring air to them, mild and muggy. Outside I recall childhood feelings, sitting in a

train for Moscow. I'm ten, eleven, thirteen. I'm travelling to
a pioneers' camp for a Soviet summer. To a lake, in a tent, on
a boat. Sometimes I also go swimming. There are lots of roll
calls, campfires, flag-waving. I don't know why this memory
suddenly crops up. This reminiscence of having spent hours
in trains travelling for an eternity. The feeling that the journey
will never end. That landscapes, places, towns pass by indif-
ferently. That every new piece of the Eastern sky makes me
feel lonelier. As if life had stopped and I was falling away into
the cosmos. Further, deeper. The feeling that the inner and
outer spaces could also be the same. Endlessness, disorientation. That's how it is. I would like to know who that person is
travelling eastwards and for whom everything seems too far,
too intangible, too big.

Magnetism. The over-extended research field that shifts along
a time curve, creates spaces to be increasingly connected, gath-
ers momentum, and that – according to the sources – could
have turned out differently. Because at the beginning there
were still contradictions. Because at the beginning some of the
actors decided to withdraw.[24] Because many doctors, scientists
and researchers in this field fled to the West. Because women
in particular refused at first. As if they had an inkling. As if they
wanted to hide and find a safe place. How is history made? I
am forced to recall Jacob again. If I visit him now, what will I
be able to tell him? Not enough, at all events. Nothing that will
bring him clarity. So wait, carry on collecting and continuing
to search.

I go to the federal archive in Finckensteinallee, Lichterfelde.
I had often been there before. In the car it occurs to me that
most of the protagonists in the files – the institute and faculty
heads, research advisers and ministers, scientists and doctors,
even the two men chosen for space flight – were from the war
children generation. Hans Haase was born in 1937, Sigmund
Jähn in 1937, Eberhard Köllner in 1939. Was East German

military research the reflection of a generation? East German space flight the symbolic image par excellence? What could the symbol have represented?

The war children of the East, the young activists as classic rebuilders most closely connected with the GDR project of hope. They are Hitler's children. They were socialized by him, marked by the cheering, victory and collective manna. Who, with this background, had to deal with the ruins after 1945. Who grew up with dead, absent or directionless parents, with untrustworthy teachers and an anxious future. Fatherless, hungry adolescents, who in the post-fascist East were carried away by the idea of a better Germany. Who moved to the new places in their blue shirts, to major construction sites, to party schools and workers' palaces. Who dreamed of community, food, security, careers and were tightly integrated in the amnesia programme of the new beginning in East Germany. Who, like no other generation, were imbued with the spirit not only of Hitler but also of Stalin. Who were caught in the grinder, in the either-or programme, in the special magnetism of violence and promise. Who, if not them, would want to fly?

Animals in silver. 26 August 1978. Sigmund Jähn was in space for almost eight days. A good week, that was to become the high point of East German space exploration, the beacon, the propaganda coup. A beacon in which nothing was left to chance. Politburo decisions, the Falke security concept, in which 250 people were checked by the security service, overall structure, general reports.[25] For the Stasi, the GDR government, military research, the great journey to the stars was an undertaking of unparalleled magnitude. The effort paid off and the mission was successful. In fact, it had a sweeter political outcome than had initially been anticipated. After the landing and return to the GDR came the mega-productions, the special programmes and editions, all orchestrated, needless to say, at the highest level. The cheering on the streets. A country in an exceptional state of mind. Three weeks later came the official reception with 1,200 guests at the Palace of the Republic in East Berlin. The high point of the celebration was the presentation for the heroic cosmonaut. A model 313, 16/7×65 R calibre double-barrelled shotgun with hunting-scene engraving and the dedication 'In memory, Erich Honecker, 21 September 1978'.[26]

'High-quality hunting engraving, animals in silver,' it says on the sheet in the archive.[27] Animals embossed on silver plate. Probably stags with elaborate antlers. You fly to the sky and the dictator ceremoniously presents you with a shotgun. I don't know why I'm fixated by this. By the hunting, by the stalking, by the male gathering, the archaic ritual of power. Scenes from the meeting of a secret society? But is it not frequently the details that hold us up in the middle of a story so as to distract us?

The body of Sigmund Jähn and the eight days in late summer 1978, for which military research in the GDR had been preparing intensively for years. In Hans Haase's postdoctoral thesis I read that for the first three days in Soyuz 31 there was only fruit juice, that the first German in space had no sense of taste and that he suffered from spatial disorientation.[28] After describing the loss of the sense of taste, Haase explained the research programme in the Jähn capsule. The previous Soyuz missions from the mid-1960s had focused mainly on the problem of weightlessness and radiation safety. The research crews had not really progressed any further.

They knew that the body could survive in weightless conditions. 'Acclimatization to the conditions of weightlessness was more rapid than the adaptation to the conditions on Earth after the flight,' it said in the debriefing after Soyuz 9.[29] But the body in space remained a tightrope-walking act. Up there it was hell. And the terrestrial body was not made for hell. To that extent, the research focus for the coming years was thus evident: 'The results of the flight urgently suggest that greater attention should be paid to the effects of weightlessness, the changed microclimate and the abnormal activities.'[30]

Radiation pharmaceuticals. It was much the same with the question of radiation safety. According to the report of the 1970 annual conference of the Interkosmos Biology and Medicine working group in Budapest, 'Most of the presentations dealt with pharmacological radiation protection.'[31] The Soviets urged the GDR people to contribute more 'so that in this way a comprehensive sub-test programme for radiation pharmaceuticals for space flight, from the molecular to the organism level, can be developed.'[32] The East Germans hesitated.

Previous experiments with conventional radiation protection had not been particularly effective.[33] Where to start? The conference also revealed a clear focus on anabolic steroids, steroidal alkaloids and glucocorticoids.[34] A short memo stated: 'Data that proves the effectiveness of anabolic steroids in connection with long-term radiation is to be noted. In irradiated animals, for example, the administration of methandrostenolone led to a statistically significant increase in erythroblastic elements in the spinal cord and spleen. According to Polish scientists, in cases of radiation sickness, anabolic steroids appear capable of preventing catabolic phenomena in the irradiated organism and of extensively normalizing DNA and RNA synthesis. This work should be extended through different radiation models to investigate in more detail the efficacy of anabolic steroids under the conditions of space flight. Research should also be initiated to determine the influence of anabolic steroids on resistance to other extreme factors of space flight.'[35]

Steroids for space? An idea that became a core aspect of military research, not least because male sex hormones could solve the problem of muscular atrophy in the 'cosmic factory'. Where there were anabolics there were also bodies. A dual effect of a sort. I wondered how that worked in practice. What was in the minds of the GDR researchers when they flew back from Budapest in 1970? Who had they been talking to? And what happened next? Anabolics would later be seen as the stuff of the Cold War. Steroids were sometimes prescribed as hormone therapy for women in the 1980s in Munich.[36] Already in the 1960s, experiments with anabolics in the GDR were not infrequently conducted in prisons.[37] Even the authorities regarded steroids as a promising stimulant. A Stasi meeting report of 10 November 1976 said of mesterolone made by Schering AG in West Berlin: 'This substance has already been administered to high-level state functionaries and leading party and GDR government cadres.'[38]

Country within a country. The mesterolone report of 10 November 1976. Six days later, the songwriter Wolf Biermann was expelled from the GDR, and on 19 November the writer Jürgen Fuchs was arrested in his car. Three dates that merge to become an expression of the feelings of the time. As if I were making my way through a country within a country, as if I were once again encountering the internal conflicts. But is it possible to be under way in this landscape and not ask the questions that have been asked so often: what happened to Jürgen Fuchs in Stasi confinement?

The use of radioactive substances and the Criminal Investigation section at Humboldt University, Berlin. 'On 911 pages under the study title "Toxdat" is a list of every conceivable way of killing a person with poison. The study lists more than 200 toxic and radioactive substances and describes in detail how they can be used,' wrote *Spiegel* journalist Peter Wensierski in his article 'In Kopfhöhe ausgerichtet'.[39] The microdoses, the radionuclides. All listed and reported. There is all kinds of evidence but no definitive proof. The fact is that Jürgen Fuchs died aged forty-eight. A fact without explanation. But why not ask again? Why not ask if the train of thought – steroids, radiation research, military research, GDR prison – has been carried through to its conclusion?

Two twenty-six. The Jähn flight and the twenty-five GDR experiments alone on board: on smoke plumes over industrial areas, on polar light, on molten glass, on dreaming, on smelling, sleeping, urinating, eating, cardiac activity, hearing thresholds, subjective sense of time, taste.[40] Also on speech. In this experiment, Sigmund Jähn had to recite the 'experimental index *two twenty-six*' whenever he made radio contact with Earth.[41] 'After taking his seat in the cockpit, in the acceleration phase during the ascent, shortly after the transition to weightlessness, immediately before, during and after the coupling manoeuvre, immediately before and after the daily physical training, immediately before the landing, during the deceleration phase, after landing.'[42] In addition, '226' was to be spoken on tape in various situations.

The experiment investigated 'psychophysical states', more precisely 'the ability to function or 'the psychological reliability' of the cosmonaut.[43] The final report summarized: 'In all stages of the flight, the emotional tension of the cosmonaut was higher than in the preflight phase, without any indication of an impairment to functioning. This tension quickly abated on landing.'[44]

Harmless? Perhaps. But a project that nevertheless looked as if it was a work in progress, as if it was still in its infancy.

Showers can be taken once a week on board the space station. A shower cabin is available for this purpose. The cosmonaut unfolds a plastic sheet from top to bottom that seals him hermetically from the outside so that no drops of water can escape. For safety reasons, the cosmonaut wears a nose clip in this cabin and breathes through a mouthpiece and tube similar to a diver's equipment.

Zentrales Archiv des Deutschen Zentrums für Luft- und Raumfahrt e.V., Göttingen, BAAR, A872, unnumbered.

Abrek and Bion

Divided space. The sweetie e-mails were almost forgotten, the unknown soldier made no further appearances. But in autumn 2018 the *Nordkurier* ran a whole series of articles about the Doping-Opfer-Hilfe and about me. A media outburst, in which the association was depicted as a 'secret society' with me as its leader. The criticisms were always the same: unethical! The tenor: falsified data, unjustified claims, subjective sense of victimhood, a self-serving enterprise for both the victims and the association. The false claims were settled in court, the criticisms proved to be groundless, but in any case it wasn't about the facts. So what then?

In 2013 the historian Christiane Baumann had published a study of the *Nordkurier* showing that the newspaper had managed to cover up its incriminating past well beyond the year 1989. The logic of the old system remained intact in this way despite the new staff. In 1989, a quarter of the editorial staff had been Stasi informers. Of the fourteen regional heads, ten had worked for the secret service in 1987. In the Neubrandenburg local editorial board, three out of four editors were unofficial Stasi collaborators.[1] The sports section, it was said, had been 'practically a Stasi outpost'.[2] For a long period, even after the end of the GDR, former Stasi journalists had been able to write for the newspaper under different pseudonyms. There was an evident continuity and a sense of subversion, yet the newspaper heads from the West felt no responsibity for this situation.[3]

The attacks on the victims' association, the stigmatization of those involved as malingerers, wimps, liars, imposters. The aspect of trauma and campaign was new to me. For years we had heard reports of suffering. Our practical experience showed that a traumatic experience could have a long-term aftermath. That there was nothing straightforward about it. That it could have acute consequences. That contradictions existed, alongside eruptive, ambiguous and irrational aspects. But this assault was something else. The loose threads, side strands and blinding flashes of the attacks. The twisted imbalance. How was an overview to be maintained? How was it possible to find a way through? How could it be understood in a way that can be retold? Not least as the *Nordkurier* still had solid support in November 2018. A quartet of supposed investigators appeared with a sixty-page pamphlet. This was not factual questions, substantive criticism or explanations, but something else. The criticisms sounded as if they had been copied from the newspaper: the fake statistics, the whiners, the unscientific approach. And now?

In my search I came across José Brunner's book *Die Politik des Traumas*, which became a key text and reference guide.[4] It helped me to understand, or at least to begin to understand, what we were dealing with and what was going on in general. Brunner, a philosopher of science in Tel Aviv who has taught at universities around the world, is known mainly for his research on trauma and its connection with social discourse. He describes trauma as 'an invisible mental causality that appears to obey laws that are not the same as what we know from physics or somatic medicine'.[5] That 'relatively insignificant events can in some cases [result in] severe symptoms' and vice versa.[6] And that the public domain is always divided on the subject of violence.[7] This was not entirely new, but it helped me. The more I read, the more I realized that two things were colliding in this staged incident: the law of physical trauma and the physics of a campaign. The traditional powerlessness of the victims and the traditional power of the perpetrators, who were confronting one another for a second time in the here and now. This made sense to me. But I didn't know how to deal with it.

Once again, a step back to briefly review the situation. Where were we? A dictatorship and its sports system, lots of victories and the dark side, more precisely State Research Plan 14.25, implemented from 1974 on between 12,000 and 15,000 athletes. It was basically about state-controlled and state-financed doping, centralized implementation concepts, research, development and confidentiality. The German Central Investigation Department for Government and Reunification-Related Crime (ZERV) began its investigations in 1993. It was very thorough. The major Berlin doping trial took place in 2000, with a unanimous verdict. The court found that the nineteen co-plaintiffs were definitely 'victims' of a 'totalitarian power structure'. The Federal Court of Justice also had to give consideration to this subject matter in the appeal. Here again the decision was clear. The Federal Public Prosecutor's Office spoke of 'centrally controlled systematic doping', a 'state-controlled and organized system' and argued that the victims had been 'manipulated by the state . . . for its own ends'.[8]

The objective offence of bodily harm. Everything was examined, legally clarified and decided in 2000. And in 2018? It looked as if this old dictatorship story, already sorted out twenty years previously, was to be rewritten once more. I didn't want to be involved in this fight all over again. For me it was dated and unnecessary. Everything that had needed explaining had been explained. The trials, the judgments, the compensation had all been settled. I decided not to stand at the association's next elections. The discussion was undignified and agonizing, particularly for the victims. I resigned. That was December 2018.

The process of coming to terms with the past is a difficult matter, it is only possible to a partial extent, it meets resistance, it is usually sobering and almost always disappointing in retrospect. That's how it is. It seems natural and inevitable. Coming to terms is a delicate process. It goes back and forth. In some cases you also have to start again from less than nothing. The year 2000 was not 2018. The collective perpetrator trauma had developed a new form over the years. GDR sport had to be justified, the system's holy grail of winning defended. A kind of identity politics. Or was it more complicated after all?

Hidden images. Spring 2019, summer 2019. Landtag elections in Saxony, Brandenburg and Thuringia. The AfD was about to have its first head of government, hijacking the 1989 revolution for its purposes. Andreas Kalbitz, Brandenburg's top AfD candidate wore white shirts. He said we are hitting a nerve. I spent as much time as I could in the archive in Freiburg. The turbulence in the East felt more like a distorted underwater noise there. A long way away, gurgling. In the evening, the long-term Italian astronaut Samantha Cristoforetti said on television: 'During the day, humanity can barely be seen from space. You can see structures. You can see deserts, mountains, craters. And also antiquity, if you look long enough. Everything is shrunken.' A refined and discriminating view.

I didn't have this view. When I tried to compare the military research records and sources using invenio, the federal archive's digital ordering system, I found gaps. Many of the classified theses were missing, or else I couldn't find them. The smiling man at the counter nodded and agreed that it was a possibility. There was still the old Argus system, he said, which was gradually being ported to the new system. But it took time. He asked for my understanding and picked up the phone. Five sentences later he said that I should go to the annex, where I would find the old file cards. I would have to sort through them myself.

I like it when archives are not just reading rooms but real spaces. When I can find out where history's toilet is located, and its coffee machine. When I can set off and explore. The corridors, the stairways, the doors, the annexes. Then I have the feeling that history has something to do with getting air. Something is in the course of opening. Things can get clearer. In the annex, three index card boxes were placed in front of me. Old wooden GDR boxes, the cards written by hand.

I was struck by the fact that some of the doctoral theses were about poison. 'Clinical picture and treatment of selected sabotage poisons'[9] or 'Antidotes to chemical weapons'.[10] Several works were about blood. 'Coagulation analysis after administration of UV-treated whole blood in rabbits'[11] or 'Experiments on the characterization and effect of blood preparations'.[12] There were a number of works about radiation: 'Combination of ionizing radiation and intoxication with model nerve agents'[13] or 'Animal experiments to determine the influence of selected antiarrhythmics on the course of acute radiation sickness'.[14] Some works were about performance: 'Performance of women and their suitability for military purposes'[15] or 'Changes in the reactivity of the immune system under the conditions of high-performance training'.[16] A surprising number of works dealt with extreme situations: 'Clinical psychological aspects of the personality of detainees in prison and custody who have swallowed foreign bodies',[17] 'On the causes and treatment of food denial in prison and custody'[18] or 'Psychiatric analysis of 100 attempted suicides'.[19]

Poison, blood, radiation, performances, extremes. Can any conclusions be drawn from all this? A pattern, a logic? Was there a plan? Was there something behind the themes? Connections? And the animals? I looked through the file cards. I noted that experiments in the 1970s focused above all on 'experimentally poisoned rats'. In the 1980s the research turned more to 'experimentally irradiated rats' or 'UV-treated whole blood in rabbits'. Did that mean anything? A paradigm shift? Maybe yes, maybe no. Speculation was useless. So carry on looking, read theses, try not to lose the thread.

Short paths. The successful GDR space mission gave a boost to Honecker's nation-building enthusiasm and once again opened up the possibility for further space research. Perhaps there was more to be done? In October 1980 the decision was adopted to form a centre for space research.[20] The new institute was founded on 1 April 1981 as an adjunct to the Academy of Sciences.[21] There was also orchestrated restructuring elsewhere: on 12 August 1981 the Council of Ministers adopted a decision to form a military medicine academy in Bad Saarow, not far from Berlin; on 11 November 1981 the Faculty of Military Medicine in Greifswald was wound up; and on 1 December 1981 the Military Medicine Academy was founded in Bad Saarow as a GDR university answerable to the Minister for National Defence.[22]

The course change happened quickly and the lines of communication were significantly shortened. It was about the bundling of resources and synergies. Military medicine, military research and the army hospital were combined in a single location in Bad Saarow. The affiliation to the Academy of Sciences in Berlin and its institutes became much more direct, and the ministries and policymakers in the capital were also reachable more quickly. Perhaps that was the bottom line: short pathways, clear hierarchies, efficiency, strict practical application, maximum impact. Two weeks after the academy was founded and before the university could start working properly, 'leading party and government comrades met [in Bad Saarow] to discuss how to transfer the research findings'.[23]

The ninety-minute drive from Berlin-Mitte, the heavy limousines, the bumpy roads, the picturesque Lake

Scharmützel, the military area buried deep among the pine trees, the sentries. The visitors were probably given a short tour of the area before dining and sitting down to discuss the issues together. What did they talk about, what was agreed, what research findings were to be transferred, how, when, why and where? What was so important in Bad Saarow on 15 December 1981 that it had to be clarified by these high-ranking officials at this secret location before Christmas?

Research order. Direct agreements, direct coordination, direct vocabulary: a rarity in the country as a whole, but standard procedure in Bad Saarow. Overnight the impossible became possible. The latest research literature from all over the world? Available within days. The most modern measuring equipment from the West? Paid for in hard currency. On 20 October 1982 an agreement was concluded regarding close coordination and interdisciplinary networking between the Military Medicine Academy, the Aerospace Medicine Institute, the Academy of Sciences of the GDR, the 'brotherly armies', and the Ministry of Health.[24]

The agendas of the faculty and plenary meetings in Bad Saarow, particularly at the beginning, were full of expert opinions, agreements and directives. The Jähn flight had given rise to a clear conclusion with regard to future research in the country: 'The findings are also of importance for medical practice and research, particularly in the field of industrial medicine and psychology, sports medicine, and military medicine.'[25] Working groups were constantly enlarged, new research projects initiated, additional structural directives incorporated. In rapid succession.

29 April 1983: 'Establishment of the conditions for a coordinated computer-assisted information system connecting the military medicine department, the Military Medicine Academy and the Institute for Aerospace Medicine.'[26]

5 May 1983: 'Inauguration of the new building for the Institute of Space Research in Berlin-Adlershof, Rudower Chaussee 5.'[27]

14 October 1983: 'Agreement with GERMED, cooperation with the Research Institute for Medical Diagnosis, definition of research aims 1986–90, blood substitutes, radiation biology, Military Medicine Academy directives, defence of Central Research Projects 18 and 19.'[28]

15 December 1983: 'Cooperation between the Research Centre for Molecular Biology and Medicine of the Academy of Sciences of the GDR and the Ministry of Health was intensified in certain areas. New cooperation partners were acquired: the VEB Pharmazeutisches Kombinat GERMED, which is very interested in working with us, and the Research Institute for Medical Diagnosis. Budget discussions will take place with the Academy of Sciences of the GDR and the Ministry of Health in the coming days. The context for these consultations is favourable.'[29]

Within a short time, Bad Saarow became the focus and driving force behind military research. The inner circle. A sky consortium of a kind. Everything seemed to come together here. The research tempo at the military academy was very rapid from the outset. In early 1984 the army general Heinz Hoffmann, head of the East German military, issued his own research order.[30] It is listed in the minutes as an additional line of approach.

Inserted. Soviet biosatellites were launched into space almost every year from 1973.[31] On board were flies and plants. From 1975 the USA and France also participated in Eastern European bio-flights. Biosputnik 1514 in 1983 was to be the next step in the large-scale biospace programme. It was launched on 14 December 1983. A day later the research coordination between Berlin, Greifswald, Bad Saarow and Königsbrück was agreed. A signal, a secret appeal, the planned synchronization between the skies and the Earth? But how to reconcile the two, how to describe it?

In an initial assessment of Biosputnik 1514, the physiologist Karl Hecht, born 1924, stated on 29 May 1984 to the Space Research Coordination Council of the GDR: 'Experiments with animals and plants in biosatellites are a fixed component of Soviet space research . . . and an integral component of the Interkosmos programme. Biosatellite experiments are designed to answer questions of importance for manned space flight but which, for humanitarian reasons, cannot be carried out on humans.'[32] Hecht was head at the time of the neuropathophysiology department of the Charité Psychiatric Clinic and was one of a growing pool of East German space research scientists. His report to the board contained detailed information about his work for Biosputnik 1514, in which two monkey cosmonauts were launched into space for the first time: 'The preparation of the monkeys for space travel was extremely difficult, because it was the first experiment of its type by the USSR . . . The transportation of the animals by plane from Sukhumi to Moscow, the new environment and a number of surgical interventions to insert electrodes meant that the animals were in a state of permanent stress.'[33]

It was this stress, Hecht explained to the members of the Coordination Council, that alarmed the Soviets. 'For that reason, the Scientific Council for Space Medicine and Biology of the USSR requested that we use substance P to increase the stress resistance of these animals.'[34] In the minutes, substance P is described as a neuropeptide consisting of eleven amino acids and was regarded as a key substance for pain, anxiety, inflammation and depression. Hecht believed this all to be a 'risky operation because there was absolutely no experience of substance P in primates'.[35] 'We nevertheless took the interest of the Soviet specialists into account and pursued the matter as an exceptional project.'[36]

What did this exception look like? The monkey farm founded in the 1920s and widely known as a research station, and eighteen monkeys selected for consideration for space travel. The two rhesus monkeys Abrek and Bion, who were finally selected for space travel together with cornseeds, crocus bulbs, three guppies and ten rats. The Sukhumi preparations and the insertions: various electrodes in Abrek and Bion, in the carotid artery and elsewhere. The injection of substance P for Abrek, and its absence in Bion. The flight of the two from Sukhumi to Moscow. The doped Abrek, whose 'electrical brain and muscle activity was measured so as to examine the sleep/ waking cycle', who quickly adapted to weightlessness and was able to complete its part of the programme without problem.[37] Bion, who only started feeding on the third day of the flight, whose 'face swelled up on the first to fourth days, as with many human cosmonauts' and who did not complete its programme.[38] Hecht's conclusions that suggested a difference in the 'findings for humans and monkeys', raising new questions for aerospace medicine: 'Are different reaction mechanisms in play for monkeys compared to humans? Are the subjective experiences of cosmonauts real or illusions?'[39]

Suitability for flight. Monkeys have been a major subject of study in recent ethnology books. As if they were finally emerging from the forest, looking at us and asking: are you sure what the roles are here? Who is telling the story? Monkeys have thus taken on a new role in field research. A project of hope whose observers are sentient beings. This cannot be said of the space ethnology of the 1980s. The research took no account of Bion's perspective. It was not planned. A gap. What would it have said if it had been allowed to do so? What would it have said of the entire undertaking in which it was chosen as a space animal?[40]

It is interesting to note how the neuropeptide research at Humboldt University in Berlin in the 1980s gradually moved away from its original position. Whereas it was agreed in

1984 that there were humanitarian reasons for not conducting research on humans, Karl Hecht sang a different tune
three years later: 'The USA is endeavouring to catch up with
and overtake the USSR in the field of medicobiological space
research . . . The *suitability for flight* of a scientific instrument
or substances and materials is therefore the criterion and aim
of every scientific project, which must be concluded as quickly
as possible.'[41] He added: 'The use of substance P in humans and
animals for space flight to expedite their adaptation to conditions in space was considered for the first time.'[42]

The biopolitical military research in the GDR in the 1980s.
They were years of synchronicity. It was about bundling,
tempo, focusing, urgent research, a 'higher level of combat
readiness'.[43] It was not a matter of synchronization between
the skies and the Earth, nor a matter of external pressure.
These were processes that were clearly decided internally.

The side facing the sun is therefore to be cooled and the shadow side is to be heated. The cosmonaut wears mesh underwear containing a capillary tube system with liquid flowing through it. The required effect is produced by suitable control of the flow.

Zentrales Archiv des Deutschen Zentrums für Luft- und Raumfahrt e.V., Göttingen, BAAR, A872, unnumbered.

Cosmic microwave background radiation

Found objects and triggers. I have to go back to it again. Jena, autumn 1980 and the film *The Serpent's Egg*. What was it about? Why is it that forty years later I can still recall my feelings when watching the film? What did I see? I buy a Bergman edition. About time. The first scenes: November 1923. People in slow motion, stumbling. Exhausted, heavy, in the second before falling. A swaying mass.

Then the story, the over-illustrated characters, the festering debacle. It doesn't move me. I look and remain outside. Why is that? And why was it different forty years ago? Because of the time that has elapsed? The feeling only changes after the ticking starts behind the wall, when the unbearable noise of the machines is added, the hard documentary scenes, the thing with the archive. Now I'm hooked, now I want to see everything in detail. Why? Is it the uneasiness that the fiction evokes? Is it the way Bergman tells the story? The fear that he hasn't made enough of what is called the vision of a time? Is it not sickening enough?

Our modern need for real time, triggers, the extreme, directness and spectacle. Against this, form as a hiding place, protection, time cap. Is the substance searching for the form or the form for the substance? And who believes they can decide? Who says what's right? Complicated again. But for the time being, perhaps the only thing is to take these questions as seriously as possible. 'How do I find my way out?' asks the main character in *The Serpent's Egg* as he rushes through the archive. It is the largest hospital archive in Europe, says a voice. I had forgotten about the archive in the film. Completely. The hermetic, the labyrinthine, the sponge rot, the catacombs of memory – I didn't remember it at all. It smelled medieval, a kind of hall of mirrors and the place for the serpent's egg idea.

The thing with the film inside and the time. Forty years. As if there were two tracks. As if it were possible to move simultaneously through two archives of feelings. As if two existences were trying to meet, to approach each other with words. As if one was taking the other's hand and leading it. But where to? The divergent currents of our time. It is mid-February 2020. A friend sends me an e-mail. It says that someone from the Stasi document authority has hacked my victim file. Documents have been photographed. They are being circulated. Reports, sources, secret service operation plans about me from 1984 and 1985. They are being sent out with many others with the subject line 'One of many found objects'.

I visit the head of the authority and demand an explanation. A friendly man sits opposite me at the table and says that it's not acceptable, it should never have happened. It affects a core area of our work. I'm glad you came. We'll look into it. It's March, May 2020, a pandemic in the country. I write letters to the authorities. I persevere. Authorities sometimes don't need or want to.

The archives in the country are not accessible. I try to organize what's on the desk. There's a lot. But where are the orders for the experiments, the agreements, the records on the New Man? Where is the essence? The unknown soldier. Perhaps he's unnecessary, I think. Perhaps there is not just one major action, perhaps it happens of its own accord, perhaps in our time.

Pampering. The early days of the Faculty of Military Medicine in Greifswald and the later space biomedicine. In July 2020 I visit the Stasi document authority in Schwerin. I want to look at the files and applied to do so a long time earlier. Will I find what I'm looking for? I arrange an appointment. The address: Resthof Leezen. The names of the towns on the way there – Görslow, Pinnow, Dobin – evoke the north, wind and sea buckthorn. The premises are in a former GDR army barracks in the middle of a field on the banks of Lake Schwerin. In front of the building a herd of weary cows. The animals are dozing. The heat affects everyone. In the reading room a table and a chair.

Opposite is a table and chair with a woman who will watch over me. You are the only person this week, she greets me, and fans herself absentmindedly. In the sky above, an aeroplane roars. The shutters rattle. The cows outside make strange noises. I look out of the window and see Schwerin Castle sparkling on the other side of the lake. The sky is almost Prussian blue.

Space research and Greifswald. The protagonists: always the same names. Those who wanted to get in obtained the necessary entry from those who were already involved – an expert opinion for a doctoral thesis. Everyone knew each other; they were scrutinized, chosen from the classes and courses in the faculty, pampered, ideologically screened. At the end the new entrants were 'approached individually'.[1] In the 'plan specifications' this was called 'creation of a reserve cadre'.[2] The whole thing seemed intimate, like a well-organized closed shop. A special nucleus.

Double binds. Socialized in the military environment, protected and legitimized by it, this nucleus gradually developed its own research culture. Two brief biographies and one typical researcher under the magnifying glass as examples of Greifswald and space and the rapid merging of military and civilian research in the 1980s. Hans Gürtler, born in 1933 in Greifswald, studied medicine in his home town and was a member from 1955 of the GDR armed forces. In 1958 he completed compulsory service as an assistant in the Central Hospital of the National People's Army in Bad Saarow. In 1960 doctorate from the Department of Medicine in Greifswald, then two years as an army doctor and specialist training in internal medicine. In 1965 transfer to the Main Political Administration in the Ministry of National Defence. From 1966 head of sports medicine there, responsible for the army sports clubs in the country and hence for 'applied elite sports research in the National People's Army and practical implementation of findings'.[3] In March 1966 information trip to Moscow to 'get to know Soviet sports medicine'. From 1967 to 1971 boxing association medical officer. In 1973 postdoctoral thesis in Greifswald, supervised by Prof. Siegfried Israel, since 1962 chief physician in Kreischa and the man who is said to have used drugs from Algeria back in the early 1960s on the Peace Race legend Täve Schur.[4] A further expert was Günter Ewert, born in 1934, professor in the Faculty of Military Medicine in Greifswald since 1973 and the man to have written the only comprehensive book about the faculty to date. Published as a cover-up text in 2015.[5]

In 1974 appointment of Hans Gürtler as deputy director of sports medicine at the Research Institute for Physical Culture and Sport (FKS). From August 1975 cooperation with the GDR state security, in 1976 as unofficial callaborator Hans Georg Meier.[6] He was a member of the classified information group (VS-Nomenklaturgruppe) at the FKS and, as the secret service notes, the person with 'the most comprehensive overview of all research subjects at the FKS'. Medical officer of the Additional Performance Reserves research group at the Research Centre for GDR State Doping.[7] In 1983 released from his function at the

FKS, 1985 disciplinary proceedings, not for political reasons.[8] Then from 1988 to 1992 ordinary professor of sports medicine, from 1994 professor of rehabilitation/sports medicine at the University of Greifswald. He died in Lubmin in 2018.

Hansgeorg Hüller, born in 1929. Attended school in Erfurt, 1949 People's Police, enrolled in the Faculty of Medicine in Leipzig, then in the Faculty of Military Medicine in Greifswald. Joined the National People's Army in 1956. In 1958 doctorate in physiological chemistry. From 1960 unofficial collaborator Walter Schmidt working for the Stasi. Research commission from the Ministry of National Defence on antidotes to chemical agents.[9] Head of the Pharmacology Institute at the University of Greifswald. From 1976 introduced to the illegal steroid drug tests by VEB Jenapharm.[10] From 1977 'collaboration as pharmacological expert in pilot studies and clinical pretrials at the FKS'.[11] In 1979 a conference organized by Hüller at the University of Greifswald 'On effects and recommendations for further use of STS (steroid substance)'.[12] The Stasi regarded Hüller as an important 'leading political liaison for all research and application activities' concerning anabolics.[13] Director of the Institute for Clinical Pharmacology at Humboldt University in Berlin, also chair of the Institute after 1989.[14] In a statement in connection with the investigation of GDR doping, Hüller wrote on 22 January 1993: 'During my decades of drug research I did not violate any laws or ethical standards of the GDR or internationally accepted scientific or ethical medical principles.'[15]

What were the internal motives for pursuing this type of career? Or rather, what could they have been? I think again of father, born in 1934. How else can I conceive it all? How were the internalized Hitler and the promised new era in the East, this life between two dictatorships, to be reconciled? East German space research is the history of our fathers. I mean that quite literally. I mean *our* and I mean *fathers*. Perhaps their history is one of defeat that had become ingrained in them and the attempt to expunge and get rid of it at any cost. Perhaps it is a generation that sought and was unable to find their fathers in the military. The vitality of the war children to put behind them the defeat they felt inside, often going too far in the attempt to do so. The effort to shrug off their fathers' guilt and the destructive elements involved – this all belongs together, I think. The lost war, which they tried obsessively to turn into a victory. So it's about shame and its denial. Perhaps that's what it is. The double bind. The story of the fathers is also the fact that it was written about. It happened. They told it. It doesn't matter what they say about it and even less what others think about it.

Degraded stars. These scientists, highly trained, with practical experience, career-driven, and initiated into the army's activities, perhaps incorporated in the secret service. Their offensive operations and the synchronicity of the 1980s. In retrospect they saw themselves as honest workers and experts, as a protected men's team devoted solely to their cause, solid and repeatedly called upon. Fathers who often spoke in their Stasi reports of 'necessary preparations in an international context',[16] of world leadership, of survival, of 'technical and technological breakthroughs',[17] of extreme vigilance. When did they ever sleep?

Mid-1980s and the mainstream image of the GDR: a complacent dictatorship, socially acceptable, perhaps a bit conservative, but at least peace-loving. Mid-1980s and the GDR's anti-SDI obsession. A kind of special military-industrial complex. Star wars, for which the East needed a solution, an escape, hand-wringing and at all costs very quickly. And at the same time the Soviet Space Exploration Programme until 2020 suddenly appeared in East Berlin.[18]

A long-term strategy, a kind of exploratory UFO into hitherto unimagined galaxies: to Venus, to Mars,[19] on questions of x-ray astronomy,[20] solar wind, the problem of gamma-ray bursts, the GRANAT observatory, the RadioAstron project with outsize telescopes, cosmic microwave background radiation and so-called 'degraded stars'.[21] At some point it imploded. The last item in the plan: 'creation of a large automated station (laboratory) on the Moon with means of transport'.[22]

I need to be careful with all this frenzy and with the words. How they manage to shift the body. How they push, press, wriggle, as if they needed more space. Or at least a different space. Cosmic microwave background radiation, degraded stars, recombinations. The computer surreptitiously transforms the term 'hidden mass' (*verborgene Masse*) into 'lost mass' (*verlorene Masse*). As if we were watching the words being left to themselves. As if they wanted to stop breathing. X-ray astronomy. Will we soon be dealing with the x-ray pictures of the words as well?

The Interkosmos programme until the year 2000 was a completely new type of idea, with which the Soviets offered their allies the possibility of leaving near-Earth space and entering into the phase of extraterrestrial research.[23] Further than far away? Was the project for 'overcoming organ-based thinking' now even more important as a result? The latest New Man, a body under extreme conditions with maximum radiation protection, until he could fly behind the sun and exist there forever? What came first – Star Wars, the War of Distance, or the War of the Latest Body? And who decided the strategy? A 1987 dossier 'On exploration of the cosmos' from the Academy of the USSR states that 'the exploration of space outside the solar system [calls for] the design of an electronic person'.[24]

In the mid-1980s the fronts seemed to be moving in different directions. A question of a new balance of power. In the 1970s, the Soviets had already entered into their first space cooperations with the West.[25] France, the USA and West Germany were particularly involved in the biosputniks. In a working report, Karl Hecht stated that 'even in 1981 the FRG specialists at the Meeting of the Commission on Gravitational

Physiology in Innsbruck recognized the superiority of GDR medicobiological space research'.[26] But that was over. Now it was: 'We were informed confidentially by the Soviets that the long-standing agreement between the USSR and the FRG on medicobiological space research is highly effective. The FRG offers the Soviet Union far more material than the GDR.'[27]

A fact that caused some dismay within the East German space consortium. The attempt by the Soviets to reorient their research axis in the mid-1980s 'based on extensive international cooperation' was entirely due to the circumstances.[28] A front shift that was not trivial but an explicit component of the Soviet Union's asymmetrical strategy. In order to survive it needed the enemy, its money and above all its better technology. Even the sky had become more complicated. How did all this impact the military laboratories in the East?

Greater attention is to be paid to ground research, which forms the basis for the development of flight programmes. Particular attention must be devoted to the application of the findings in practical healthcare in our states (hospitals, sport).

Extract from the international cooperation plan 1981/1982, chapter 'Cosmic physiology', Zentrales Archiv des Deutschen Zentrums für Luft- und Raumfahrt e.V., Göttingen, BAAR, A823, unnumbered.

Suitable ground models

Escalated. Apart from Abrek and Bion in Biosputnik 1514 launched in December 1983, there was also Tevton.[1] Like the other two rhesus monkeys, it was prepared in Sukhumi for its cosmonaut existence but was also used at the same time on the ground as a control animal.[2] 'Using the method of instrument-triggered reflex (operator activity) with food rewards, the higher neural activity was examined in the monkeys Abrek and Bion (space animals) and Tevton (control animal) before and during the flight, and on the first day, first week and third week after the flight.'[3] The preferred food reward was sea buckthorn juice. Otherwise, Tevton remained stuck in its capsule waiting for its colleagues to end their space mission.

Above all, however, the ground cosmonaut Tevton was destined for research with substance P, a neuropeptide that was to be used 'as a means of increasing individual stress resistance'.[4] One report stated: 'The effect of intravenous substance P was tested on twelve monkeys in high-stress situations, as a result of which the entire higher nervous system had broken down.'[5] The thing with words. Twelve monkeys, all of which broke down? Not five, not eight, but all? What was that? What was meant here by stress? Was it not rather sheer panic? Twelve animals in deathly fear? Because that's what it was. Just that. But what did a total collapse in monkeys look like? Anger, aggression, fear, trembling? When do these large animals stop struggling? And why did they have names, when the plan was to drive them crazy? Why personalize them for the terrible sensations to come? To make them as human-like as possible? To bridge the gap between man and animals?

'The tests revealed that in all animals SP 1–11 fully restored ... the reduced ability to work. There was an increase in intensity and length of performance, improved concentration, learning ability and motor coordination.'[6] The primate research for Biosputnik 1514 became the paradigm for future space biomedicine. International cooperation, maximum results, clear research advances – these were the prerequisites for a successful operation. The East Germans had already chalked up 'world-ranking contributions' regarding 'acute and chronic extreme situations (escalated emotional stress) and their compensation or adaptation mechanisms'.[7] The assessment of the flight was unanimously euphoric, even by the Soviets: 'In total, the Soviet colleagues estimate that their experiments on the utility of substance P in the primate Biosputnik experiments have been multiply confirmed and that the preliminary work by the GDR on substance P is extremely useful for it.'[8]

Tumbling. Capsule animal Tevton became an image: ground monkey under brutal stress, with its will extinguished, receiving its drugs and then performing the programme. Laboratory monkey Tevton became a symbol: the non-flyer, the terrestrial control animal that was experimented on to advance an ideology.[9] Tevton the substitute programme, the diversion, the surrogate, in which the planned experiments were to be located.[10]

Ground monkey Tevton also provides the clue to the 'model experiments on Earth'.[11] Aspects such as 'the ability of the organism to withstand extreme acceleration', 'the influence of pharmacological substances on vestibular function', 'symptoms of tumbling' and repeatedly 'weightlessness'.[12] It was about the 'influence of pharmacological substances on the functional state of the organism under changes in the gas milieu', 'genetically fixed changes', 'breeding of resistant creatures'.[13] Throughout the entire East, Interkosmos research teams attempted to remap the extremes of human existence. They sought a superlative version: the most accelerated body, the coldest, most heat-stressed, most undemanding, strongest, most exhausted, most disoriented, loneliest, most stressed, the most wrecked.

The research reports state: 'The coldness tests (24-hour exposure at 12 degrees) by the specialists from the People's Republic of Poland are of particular interest. Unfortunately, such experiments are used extremely rarely, although they are much more informative than acute short-term tests, because they allow a thorough investigation of the organism's reserves when exposed to particular effects.'[14] Or: 'Damage situations are simulated in animal experiments with a view to investigating the effect of low oxygen and high carbon dioxide concentrations due to the failure of the regeneration system in the hermetic capsule.'[15]

Extreme acceleration, coldness tests, reserves, damage situations. The records and reports of the Interkosmos biomedical research are a narrative in their own right of how research scenarios, topics and experimental equipment aimed at a clear target: the maximum 'work capacity and physical reliability of the cosmonaut'.[16] To that end, fitness for space travel was constantly demanded. To that end, ground experiments were adapted to the 'conditions of space flight'.[17] To that end, 'an important requirement for consideration of the diagnostic and therapeutic issues was their practical implementation in space medicine.'[18]

Separate budget item. On 19 December 1983, the head of the National People's Army Medical Service met with the director of the Central Institute for Molecular Biology and Medicine to review the research that had been conducted in 1982 and 1983 and to set the agenda for the following two years. It contained 'seven focuses'. One of them stated that 'the Institute for Aerospace Research in Königsbrück will be involved in the research (substance P)'.[19] According to the minutes of the next meeting, 'the Academy of Sciences insists that the research conducted by the Research Centre for Molecular Biology and Medicine and the Military Medicine Academy should not only be planned bilaterally but should also be included in the budget as a separate item under the vice-president of the Academy of Sciences'.[20]

Separate agendas, special quotas, systematic restructuring, secret agreements. The men at the tables who presumably assumed that they could define their own individual categories. Who wanted to fly together, to lift off into space, to complete their life projects. By the early 1980s, biomedical space research had acquired a good deal of knowledge as a result of the various manned flights and biosputniks. The researchers now knew more about the body in space, in particular its weak points and the failures and anomalies that could occur during space flight. The flights had also become safer and longer. It was possible to think ahead. And suddenly the tone of the new bioprogramme documents became markedly different. They started to mention individualization. Individual dosage, individual food, individual time management, individual research series. To ensure this, the plans now explicitly called for more 'suitable ground models'.[21]

'The selection of cosmonauts and the recommended prophylactic measures to avoid the influence of space travel must take account of the individual characteristics of the persons involved. This does not mean that the existing plans are unsuitable, but rather they need to be refined and supplemented. This can be done by revising the procedures and methods carried out on the ground.'[22]

State of affairs. December 2020. The talk is still of the data leak in the Stasi document authority. Since March I had been receiving regular status reports. 'We take the state of affairs described by you very seriously and will investigate the background to it,' they say.[23] We 'fully understand your annoyance,' they say.[24] We are 'conducting a thorough and comprehensive investigation of the matter at the level of department heads,' they say.[25] 'Our investigations will continue in the coming weeks,' they say.[26]

There should be no doubt about the seriousness of the investigation. Nor was there any. The authorities wanted to know and didn't abandon the investigation. It was just a matter of time. Then the results in December: the document theft did not take place during the regular processing of a task by the authority, it said. There was no written order, no written record, it said. But the file had been ordered from the outside and then viewed internally, it said. It was ordered in Gera on 13 December 2019 and delivered by courier to Berlin four days later, it said. The original had evidently been placed on a table in the office and photographed, it said.[27] The offenders were from within the department, it said.

Everything completely factual. Quite clear. And then? What happened next? I tried to imagine the situation: an authority that administers the documented fate of people in a dictatorship. A special institution, unique in the country. With people in it today who were repeating what had been recorded in the documents in their charge: hidden actions, dual strategies, collusions. Because that's what it was. Ordering files from the outside so as to misuse them inside, then covering up the traces, then not having any recollection. There were thus people in this particular institution who continued to use the methods of a dictatorship or were starting to use them again. More elaborately, of course, more camouflaged, more cleverly than had been necessary before. But it was going on. What a performance, I thought. What for? How did the past dovetail with the present? Where were the links? What belonged together and what was separate? And who in this country needed an explanation for these actions? And above all, how?

On 18 December 2020, the Stasi document authority filed a criminal complaint with the public prosecutor's office in Berlin against unknown persons. It wrote: 'In our view there are specific indications providing a basis for identifying a perpetrator. The investigations by the public prosecutor's office are of great importance for the Federal Commissioner for State Security Records (Bundesbeauftragter für die Unterlagen der Staatssicherheit – BStU). The matter in question concerns the BStU's core activities. It could permanently damage the trust of victims of Stasi injustice in the work and reputation of the authority.'[28]

All-purpose lubricant. Peptide research at the Aerospace Medicine Institute in Königsbrück. Where Jacob had been as well. Peptide research in space. Peptide research at Humboldt University in Berlin. Where and on who else? Was the escalated research with Tevton just the beginning? And how did it proceed from there? Who else was research carried out on? Initial experiments with peptides took place as early as the late 1960s, in GDR competition sport. At first, the substances were used above all in gymnastics, ice skating and shooting.[29] When the Additional Performance Reserves research group was established at the secret Research Institute for Physical Culture and Sport (FKS) in Leipzig on 16 January 1975, three main pharmaceutical research projects were defined: bioenergy, strength enhancement, and improving learning processes.[30] Winfried Schäker was responsible for the third area. A Leipzig Stasi report mentions in this regard: 'The neuropeptide oxytocin (B17) was examined between 1976 and 1980 in laboratory experiments and in training and competitions (summary results are contained in Dr Schäker's postgraduate thesis).'[31]

Winfried Schäker (1937–2021) defended his research thesis 'Improvement in central nervous and neuromuscular function and sport-specific performance through oxytocin' on 18 June 1980 as usual in Bad Saarow.[32] His supervisors included Hans Gürtler and Hansgeorg Hüller. The thesis starts with the sentence: 'As a result of tests with cats and rats, myself and athletes, the following problems were identified.' It concludes: 'From practical observation of performance development, a need to try out combinations of drugs was identified. This included the testing of the combined use of oxytocin and synthetic androgens and of beta receptor blockers.'[33]

Schäker's thesis documented research on seventeen gymnasts, fourteen track and field athletes, sixteen shooting sport athletes, three high-board divers and twenty-five wrestlers.[34] He himself noted: 'The intra-individual comparison and analysis of small groups of subjects to determine the effect of the hormone was necessary and scientifically valid.'[35] If Schäker is to be understood, the peptide research underwent an early stage of intra-individualization. 'Suitable ground models' appear to have been identified without further ado and to have been unscrupulously exploited.

In late November 1981, a scientific conference on neuropeptides took place at the Newa hotel in Dresden. The pharmaceutical group GERMED, 'as a company specializing in substances influencing memory', had been invited to report on its latest findings.[36] The meeting in Dresden was classified as confidential and thus top secret, with admission by personal invitation only.[37]

The step was finally taken in 1982 and must have come as a reaction to a top-level political demand. It required that 'research work be started as rapidly as possible' and emphasized the importance of speed.[38] A strategy that legitimized the project and allowed those involved to disregard any scientific research or ethical scruples. According to the government in Berlin, the new approach directly linked 'the political aims of the scientific and technical capacities of the Academy of Sciences with those of top-level sport'.[39] A strange quote. Nowhere else was the connection between Interkosmos and top-level sport expressed so explicitly. Elsewhere the two were kept apart, or the research documents were encrypted or destroyed, or agreements made orally.[40] The secret research at the Leipzig FKS was also specially secured and had to be destroyed: 'In consultation with the state department heads concerned, it was decided to considerably reduce the number of documented research results (300 confidential documents from State Research Plan 14.25 have been destroyed at the FKS).'[41]

A good year later, on 23 November 1983, Schäker reported that the Berlin Institute for Substance Research had offered the neuropeptide substance P 'to Dynamo for testing'.[42] Before that the report said: 'The army sports club should be supplied separately from Bad Saarow (also through its own pharmacy).'[43] Now everything was out in the open: 'Prof. Hecht will be involved in the project. He will or has already passed on substance P to the Soviet Union cosmonaut department. The information comes from Hüller in the strictest secrecy.'[44] The ranks had closed. Research centres in various locations were now in direct contact, and the boundaries, if they still existed at all, had become porous. Cooperation within the system. Neuropeptides, the all-rounders, the all-purpose lubricant – to combat anxiety, pain, fatigue, desynchronization in space, to handle extreme stress, to improve concentration, to facilitate learning. Wherever it took place, the GDR peptide research was the perfect success story, a durable bestseller, made possible over the years with all kinds of state funding and developments. How to put it succinctly and make it even clearer?

The Stasi report noted that at the Institute for Clinical Pharmacology at Humboldt University in Berlin, and hence under the supervision of Hansgeorg Hüller, 'the newly developed pharmaceutical was investigated experimentally and passed on secretly for drug testing. In this way knowledge of its planned use in competition sport can be avoided.'[45] A subsequent report noted that the use of neuropeptides in competition sport would continue to be tested 'in coordination with the Institute for Aerospace Medicine. Existing information relating to aircraft pilots is to be used to prevent signs of fatigue and to increase concentration.'[46]

Is all of this emphasis on detail really necessary? Yes, it is. It is unavoidable. It has to be specified. Otherwise it can't be seen. The researchers, the drive, the places, the secret networks, their explicit rules. Research in a dictatorship as a complex interaction between ideology and academia. The ideology legitimizes it, the academics accept it to make it their own – a story created through pressure, career ambition, competition between researchers and research institutes, an obsession with performance, fear, compulsion, dependence and often very personal researcher profiles. As far as peptides are concerned, the story clearly starts with one person, Winfried Schäker. In this case, the research became established in early GDR competition sport, linked up with civilian Academy research and then raised to a new level in the Interkosmos research. It was usually the other way round. Usually military research came first and was then used for non-military purposes. But a prestige project like Interkosmos was not a routine case. There was not a single pattern, a linear pathway. It was a Mikado system. Where necessary, the military consortium gained access through lines of communication and the secret service. The country was small, the research teams known to the decision-makers. The acquisition and protection of the research needed for space was the single clear driving force.

World class. Rats were also on board Biosputnik 1514 along with Abrek and Bion. A report on the experiments stated: 'Tests were carried out on embryonal development and postnatal ontogenesis in rats. Reproductive capability was tested on ten female rats inseminated on Earth and in the thirteenth to eighteenth days of gestation during the flight. This gestation period is very important in terms of embryonal development.'[47] A significant increase in trace elements such as iron and magnesium was noted in the animals in space. The researchers interpreted this as 'indication of an adaptation to weightlessness to protect the foetus'.[48] A loss of trace elements was noted in the control group on Earth. The baby rats in space also showed 'a considerable drop in important minerals' fifteen days after their birth.[49]

Like the shock research on Abrek, Bion and Tevton, the rat research in Biosputnik 1514 became a reference model. A highly promising result that kept on generating variants, series and completely new experimental approaches. As with the monkey experiments, the Department of Neuropathophysiology at Humboldt University played the lead role. After the success of the Biosputnik 1514 mission, follow-up projects were not long in coming. Just four months after Abrek and Bion landed, Karl Hecht, head of the Department of Neuropathophysiology, made a handwritten list of research tasks.[50] The orders came exclusively from state authorities: the Council of Ministers of the GDR, the Academy of Sciences of the GDR, the Ministry of Higher Education, the Ministry of Health, and the Ministry of Public Education. The research could not have been more state-driven. The new task for the researchers called for 'physiological, biochemical and pharmacological processes in embryonal development and in adult age under terrestrial and space conditions'.[51] As for the level of scientific research, Hecht wrote in his flourishing hand simply: 'world class'.[52]

Biosputnik 1667 was launched into space in July 1985. In direct preparation for this flight, various ground experiments, including tests on rats, were carried out with a focus on hypo-kinesis. 'As part of a research programme on life under extreme conditions, tests were carried out on the reactivity of the mineral metabolism to various powerful short-term stress factors,' said the report.[53] The set-up: 'Male Wistar rats were put under extreme stress through two hours of swimming or two hours of restraint. Immediately afterwards, the brain, liver, kidneys and extensor and flexor muscles of the hind legs, femur and hair were removed and the concentrations of ten elements in them . . . determined.'[54]

Restrained then killed and their bodies presented for dissection. It's about the animals, but it's also about the act itself. A kind of overkill. The file copies on my desk are overpopulated with Japanese quails, mice, pigs, dogs, rabbits, guppies, rats and monkeys. A brief reference in the minutes of the Military Medicine Academy faculty meeting in Bad Saarow on 24 February 1988: 'Considerable increase in costs for test animals'.[55]

I think I need to take a break.

The Soviets presented the experimental programme to examine the embryonal development of rats. Particular attention was paid to the mother/embryo relationship. Experiments on the effects of jolts and vibration in various stages of gestation showed no fundamental changes.

Memo of consultation with Prof. Gasenko, Moscow, on Interkosmos life science experiments, 29 February 1982, Zentrales Archiv des Deutschen Zentrums für Luft- und Raumfahrt e.V., Göttingen, BAAR, A852, unnumbered.

We are the first

Tangled sources. I no longer remember when the archive was open and when it was closed during the COVID-19 pandemic. At all events, it took a long time to obtain files. There were waiting lists of over a year for the reading room in the federal archive in Finckensteinallee, Berlin. At some point, the state archive in Schwerin was added to my small network of archives. It contained the files of the Central Investigation Department for Government and Reunification-Related Crime (ZERV). I commuted between Freiburg, Berlin and Schwerin, depending on where I could get a seat in the reading room. And then I had a piece of good fortune. In the Academy archive on Gendarmenmarkt, the woman from the counter came up to me one day with a fat binder. She said that she didn't know what was in it but thought it might be of interest to me.

I opened the binder. In it was a detailed list of the material I had long been looking for: Academy of Sciences, Berlin-Adlershof, Institute for Space Research, Interkosmos research department. This is it, I realized immediately. I noted the shelf numbers on my computer, left the reading room and while still on the street called the mobile phone number on the first page of the binder. It was the Institute's switchboard. A young, very direct woman's voice answered: Yes, no, I don't know, of course I'll ask, I'll call you back. Two weeks later I was sitting in the library in Adlershof, now the German Aerospace Centre. Rows of files in grey boxes on two trolleys. What are you doing here, asked a slender, efficient woman. No one has been here before about biomedicine, not for thirty years.

The days in Adlershof. The minutes, contracts, work reports, statements, research plans, consultations, agreements, documents, assessments, processing, annual work plans. A plethora of material. It was like hacking a way through the undergrowth, swinging through the past. How was I to sort and categorize it? I was alone in the basement library and looked out of the window. At eye level I could see feet: trotting, strolling, skipping, walking leisurely, stumbling. Some stopped to contemplate. You could see this in the shoes. They pointed upwards or outwards, flexed themselves like a wrinkled forehead. The march of history. From the basement library what we call history felt more like no man's land. Unobserved, forgotten, slipped away. And maybe that's how it was. Perhaps history often didn't listen at all. Perhaps it wasn't receptive, not there. Perhaps it couldn't manage. The basements of history, the old voices, the protagonists of a great communal life's work, the collective mind of a state-approved complicity that had sometime taken concrete form. Was it that? Is that what it was about? Was it about individual motives or a communal enterprise, a core? Or several cores?

National responsibility. On 8 February 1985, Heinz Hoffmann, head of the East German military, wrote to the prime minister: 'Esteemed Comrade Stoph,' he began, 'In view of the current development of the Interkosmos work . . . I would ask you to see that the Academy of Sciences of the Ministry of Health is given responsibility for pursuing the work of the Standing Working Group on Cosmic Biology and Medicine. The cooperation on the project of the members of the National People's

Army will, of course, remain in place. With socialist greetings, Hoffmann, army general.'[1]

So the military wanted to hand over control of Interkosmos biomedicine, even though the research consortium had long been working in a network? Why? Was it about people who were not to be trusted? Or even closer research synapses? Or a completely new direction? Hoffmann's letter sounded as if it had been secretly arranged. 'It is not about some kind of restaffing but the complete takeover of all national and international organizational, planning and financing operations, including the transfer to the Academy of Sciences of the GDR of space medicine contracts concluded by the National People's Army with industrial companies.'[2]

It was all accepted without objection three months later.[3] With effect from 1 January 1986, the Academy of Sciences of the GDR assumed 'national responsibility for space biology and medicine within the Interkosmos programme'.[4]

Did the new national responsibility also signify new directives? The files from this time speak a lot about 'research breakthroughs' and 'key technologies'. An 'assessment within the Interkosmos programme' gives an indication of the future direction of biomedicine: 'Further research and use of space, the creation of space stations and future interplanetary flights make necessary a completely new system of healthcare.'[5] The plans for the next years included the Medilab medical space laboratory designed to permit 'examinations on all priority areas of space medicine'.[6]

The larger sky was one thing, the difficult move to the Academy of Sciences of the GDR another. Relations between East and West Germany might have played a role as well. After long and wearing negotiations, the Agreement on Cultural Cooperation between East and West Germany, including scientific cooperation, was signed on 6 May 1986.[7] It was not really conceivable that future collaborators from West Germany would sit at a table and make agreements with representatives of the East German military. For the new status quo politics, there was therefore a need for suitable, solid, traditional negotiating tables and platforms. The GDR regime styled itself as peace-loving; it hoped to be able to orchestrate a new image for itself; and it required lots of hard currency. To that end the 'principle of foreign exchange acquisition for the import of investment goods' was established.[8] It was a matter of holding onto power. In fact, the Academy of Sciences and hence the civilian sector had a portfolio for redimensioning or commercial utilization of GDR research that was quite simply more in line with the times. A highly sensitive field that was often enough also a question of option agreements and licences.[9]

In the background, however, 'immaterial and material export' also played a not insignificant role. The Berliner Import-Export-GmbH (BIEG) was already established in the 1970s. It handled 'special requirements' – shoes, electronics, household appliances, but also 'technical services'. The study *Testen im Osten* states: 'In the framework of "immaterial exports", BIEG concluded financing agreements regarding contract clinical trials. In the 1980s it also dealt on behalf of the Ministry of Health with blood products ("material exports"). From 1985 to 1989 it earned profits of 872 million foreign exchange marks.'[10]

New markets, new players, new research alliances, the New Man as East-West win-win model? A lot of hard currency earned with the blood of its own citizens? Is there any documented evidence?

Flow properties. The thing with blood, which by the early 1980s at the latest had become a major object of research. Blood is needed for space, in cancer research, in hospitals, in the military, also for competition sport. I am reminded of Astrid, sitting in the advice centre for sports victims and absentmindedly stroking the vein in her left arm as if to try to get rid of an old pain. Blood out, blood in, again and again, she said flatly. This constant fiddling. It's good for you, they said if I asked. Everyone's doing it. The thing with blood and how the words in the files turn into memories. The young women in white overcoats standing with their little bags in the indoor arena to take blood after every sprint. The squeaking of shoes on the red tartan track, the sorting of tubes, the sick rooms in the training camps, the Petri dishes, the metallic tinkling of the appliances, the doctor's voice, the grey plastic sheet on the stretcher, and the strange moment between inside and outside, when the blood dripped into the thin tube.

The Military Medicine Academy in Bad Saarow, which in the mid-1980s signed a 'business contract with the Academy of Sciences of the GDR' concerning the 'implementation of military technical research and development projects' such as 'fluorocarbon blood substitute'.[11] The Military Medicine Academy, which regularly had secret dissertations written about the research into blood, in particular in connection with Central Research Project 14.[12] The Military Medicine Academy, which organized scientific forums on the subject of blood, such as the Fifth Saarow Symposium on Blood Purification in Military Medicine by the Detoxification Working Group in September 1989.[13] In Bad Saarow, blood was an absolute core brand.

In 1982, Manfred von Ardenne presented the substance Oxygenabund at the Dresden Research Institute, which increased the oxygen potential of blood.[14] The man from the Weisser Hirsch district of Dresden recommended his 'Ardenne pill' particularly for elderly persons and explicitly for competition athletes. Blood specialists from the research and rehabilitation facility in Kreischa quickly travelled the 20 kilometres to consult with the *éminence grise* in Dresden. A secret report in the early 1980s on UV radiation of blood stated that this method was very popular in the Soviet Union. After head of state Brezhnev had been treated with it, the experts sought out the relevant documentation and consulted Ardenne.[15] The Interkosmos bodies also talked regularly with Ardenne and involved him in their projects. In the early 1980s in particular, there were plans for the development with him of a mass spectrometer for respiratory gas analysis.[16]

On 25 June 1986, a research meeting took place in the Dynamo Berlin sports hotel on improving oxygen supply.[17] Only those with the necessary security clearance were invited, and the group was therefore small. There were just six speakers: from the Schwerin blood donor centre, the Berlin Institute for Medical Physics and Biophysics, the Berlin blood donor centre, the Academy of Sciences Institute for Molecular Biology in Berlin, the Military Medicine Academy in Bad Saarow, and the Clinic for Sports Medicine in Berlin-Buch.[18] According to a 1989 Stasi report, a research group was investigating substances 'that occur naturally in the human organism and can be isolated. Substances such as erythropoietin, a hormone that stimulates haematopoiesis, are possible alternatives.'[19] In short, erythropoietin (EPO) had now arrived in GDR competition sport.

Clinical drug trials on EPO were carried out from 1988 through the West German pharmaceutical companies Boehringer-Mannheim and Cilag in at least sixteen GDR hospitals, including clinics in Schwerin and Rostock. The trials concerned the 'clinical investigation of genetically modified erythropoietin' and 'efficacy and safety of recombined human erythropoietins'.[20] The success of the EPO hormone, initially developed for kidney diseases, was also made possible by new gene technologies used after 1984, when rEPO was developed. They had the advantage of being much safer than synthetic substances. EPO, GH, IGF-1 and insulin – modern substances for the modern body – were soon being made using entirely new methods. And the GDR? It was not required to develop anything. The West and its latest research came to it. It needed only to watch and carry on developing.

The other script. I didn't know that campaigns are scripted. That they have rules and regulations. That they employ a 'technique of confusion'. That it is possible to know today what is going to be written about you in tomorrow's newspaper. I had no idea. In the book *Die Kunst des Miteinander-Redens* by Bernhard Pörksen and Friedemann Schulz von Thun, I read that the procedure is basically quite simple.[21] The first campaign script, they say, was written by the US tobacco industry in the 1950s. The cigarette moguls at the time wanted to conceal knowledge from the public about the harmfulness of nicotine and thought up some useful ways of doing just that. This turned into a long-term campaign lasting several decades and involving huge investments. Not a nice thought.

In its modern version the strategy is as follows: (1) attack those who represent the party to be eliminated – the established voices, experts and institutions; (2) construct an alternative milieu with dossiers, press conferences, open letters and your own network in order to simulate scientific rigour and create a climate of disinformation; (3) inundate the classic media with the orchestrated controversy and appeal to fair and balanced reporting – it should be possible to find a couple of hapless journalists or ones who operate media in your interests; (4) manipulate the mass of social media and anything else that could sow further seeds of doubt; (5) exploit the general confusion to divert the discussion and promote your own interests in the ensuing chaos.[22]

Bewilderment is a vague word. Depending on where in the script it is meant to occur, it can be liberating, slippery, revealing, weak or also disruptive. On 19 May 2021, an article entitled 'The doping legend: for ideological reasons GDR sport was systematically discredited in the Federal Republic of Germany' in *Rubikon*, a political blog described by the *Süddeutsche Zeitung* as a 'cross-cutting magazine'. An article whose tone and content were familiar: supposedly 'questionable' figures, 'free loaders', 'processing industry', 'victim lobby'.[23] Nothing new there, I thought, just the author, Gerd Machalett (born 1937). His biography at the end of the article reads: 'Specialist in transfusion medicine, director of the Institute for Clinical Chemistry, Haematology and Transfusion Medicine at the Military Medicine Academy (MMA) in Bad Saarow, consultant physician for transfusion medicine to the head of the Medical Service of the National People's Army, director of the Schwerin blood donor institute.'[24]

I skim over the text. What a coincidence. As if the past and the present were facing up to one another and falling into each other's arms. Was that the explanation for the campaign? Was sport the divining rod for the space behind it that was to be concealed or hushed up? Was someone being used as a stool pigeon, or did he lay out the evidence himself? Was the article such a triumph because they had managed to stay under the radar for thirty years and because no one could point a finger anymore? Who is the *unknown soldier*? The other script? Gerd Machalett was one of the six men invited to the secret blood meeting at the Dynamo Berlin sports hotel on 25 June 1986. He was the first speaker on the agenda, given ten minutes to introduce the subject.[25] There is no record of what he actually said, but the doctor and colonel Machalett is to be encountered repeatedly in the last three years of the Bad Saarow archive.

He states himself that in the early 1960s he was the first military doctor to train as a National People's Army pioneer diver and was later responsible for the 'medical care of military divers'.[26] He also claimed 'knowledge of military toxicology' and was trained 'for twenty-five years in diagnosis and treatment of possible chemical warfare victims'.[27] Gerd Machalett, from 1973 to 1982 at the Military Medicine Academy in Bad Saarow, 'sworn to secrecy' there, fully briefed as 'member of the Scientific Council' on the ongoing research projects, 'head of the clinical haematology laboratory at the Army Hospital and member of the blood investigation research group'.[28] A military diver, a specialist in toxins and blood, basically a chemistry all-rounder, who even today is still ready to offer up excuses and make public statements about his specialist knowledge.[29] For example, when it comes to 'blood collection in GDR prisons to acquire hard currency' or the poisoning of Sergei Skripal and Alexei Navalny.[30] There also appears to be close connections with the old networks of East German competition sport.[31]

But how was it thirty or forty years ago? The striking parallels in the careers of Hans Gürtler, Hansgeorg Hüller and Gerd Machalett. The war children, comprehensively trained by the military, shaped and at some point sent back into civilian life on special missions. Did they feel selected or rejected? In their minds, were the retired colonels still members of the military? What kind of long-term effects does a secret research career leave? No publications, no speeches, no outwardly visible career ladder, no patents, no success bonuses, at most a couple of military medals?[32] Gerd Machalett appears in the files above all in connection with 'suggested measures to increase the effectiveness of auxiliary substances'.[33] The term 'auxiliary substances' is a euphemism for the doping substances in GDR sport. The Military Medicine Academy appears to have dispatched its haematologist to the blood donor centre in Schwerin in 1982 for a major research project. According to a Stasi report in January 1986: 'Dr Machalett will continue his research on competition sport through the Academy of Sciences and have access for necessary initial experiments to members of the National People's Army. . . . The aim of the research is to avoid the need for an exchange of blood through the use and activation of existing substances.'[34]

Academy of Sciences, Military Medicine Academy, Ministry of Health and competition sport.[35] With so much consolidated expertise, the project could quickly move forward. Initial consultations, then specific actions. Just a few days later, the report reads, Machalett 'is to be included in the specific research on auxiliary substances'.[36] An inquiry was made whether he was 'still currently sworn to secrecy'.[37] Traces in the archives of military colonel Machalett go beyond 1989. His name is also linked with a further major blood research project.[38] The fact is that as a poison and doping specialist, he belonged to the inner circle of East German military research. His media reputation today is all the more remarkable as a result.

Foreign bodies. Does my report end here? Are past and present aligned, strolling hand-in-hand into the sunset like two happy clones? Without a break, without an interruption, in the billowing whiteness of history? Not quite. Not yet. There is still the question of what exactly was involved in the research carried out after 1986 within the Interkosmos programme and what was meant by the national responsibility of the Academy of Sciences. It is as if the words wanted suddenly to take off on their own. As if they wanted more traction, to step on the gas, grab the steering wheel. They want to be full of meaning in themselves. I don't want that. I want evidence, footnotes. I want the narrative to be stable and rooted. I think of Jacob, Astrid, Johanna, Karla and all the others.

Summer 2021. I travel again to Freiburg. I plan to read two confidential dissertations every day. Perhaps I've missed something. What theses and studies were presented and approved at the faculty meetings in Bad Saarow? What was the justification? I note the topic of 'GDR military research and prisons', a field of research pursued intensively in the 1980s. There must also have been reasons for that. To the outside, in particular on account of the prospering business of buying freedom to emigrate to the West, the image was projected of supposed 'criminals' being imprisoned in compliance with the law. Internally, however, it was about the smooth running of the prison machinery. Sick or irregular inmates were deemed to disrupt the routine and had to be dealt with.[39]

In the confidential thesis 'Problems of the reintegration of a group of mentally ill recidivists sentenced to imprisonment under section 249 of the Criminal Code for crimes against the state,'[40] I read: 'The definition and significance of the punishment is determined in our legal system as a function of its class relevance, thereby demonstrating its superiority over punishments in an exploitative society. ... The punishment has thus a progressive revolutionary character.'[41]

I read: 'Psychiatric analysis of 100 suicide attempts by prisoners.'[42] I read: 'On the personality of persons swallowing foreign bodies in prisons and custody.'[43] I read: 'The alcoholic in GDR prisons.'[44] I read: 'On the causes and treatment of food denial in prisons.'[45] I read: 'Recording and evaluation of abnormal behaviour by prison inmates.'[46] I read: 'On the sexuality of male prisoners.'[47]

The locations: Leipzig prison hospital, Neustrelitz prison, Waldheim prison, Berlin prison. The 'patients' – almost one hundred inmates. All of the works defended in Bad Saarow.[48] The file landscapes. The storage locations. How was it? The tables, the rooms, the topics, the strategic meetings, the defences. What was put in the files and what was omitted? But couldn't the GDR prisons have been a 'suitable ground model' for space research? Don't 'extreme research' in space and in the encapsulated cells of a prison have a lot in common? Was it not a question in both cases of when the body tilts? The determination of the limits to an extreme situation?

I order photos from the archive. Perhaps they will tell me something. On the pictures: some fifty military personnel with rows of medal ribbons as newly appointed members of the Scientific Council. A crowded room for an official speech by army commander-in-chief Heinz Hoffmann. Graduations, award ceremonies, student cohorts. Lots of polyester and even more rubber plants. A colonel and the president of the Academy of Sciences at a massive oak table discussing the result of blood substitute research.[49] The people met regularly, discussed and enthusiastically exchanged their ideas. What did they learn from one another? The actual results, the latest strategies, the research drive for the future space scenario?

Growth plates. Perhaps enough has been said: the blue tablets, the deep voices, the star performances, the wearisome follow-up stories. The subject of GDR military research and sport. But how did it all begin? When did military matters and sport converge? Who set up the connections? An early document in the run-up to the 1964 Olympic Games in Tokyo: Hans Schuster (1928–2009), director of the research department at the German University of Physical Education (DHfK) in Leipzig and later long-standing head of the FKS, reported as a Stasi informer that the substances used in competition sport at this time 'only had a positive effect in endurance disciplines (long-distance running, cycling, rowing)'.[50] This did not apply for power disciplines, where only 'strychnine-based [substances], which therefore did not provide an immediate effect', were used.

The author considered this to be unacceptable and demanded that the secret service conduct a 'general inquiry' to ensure that GDR sport did not 'fall behind'. He also made a few specific suggestions. The most important thing was to develop 'an unofficial system with a few reliable scientists who worked outside the sports milieu'.[51] To promote his idea he met Stasi boss Erich Mielke in Leipzig in summer 1964 and received a positive response.[52] They got on well and had the same interests. 'At the meeting, the Comrade Minister stated that he would support the testing of certain substances within his own organization.'[53] The meeting led to a secret connection that lasted twenty-five years. For Mielke, Schuster became a trusted contact in Leipzig, a branch of the Bad Saarow operation. Schuster submitted ideas and information, and with the support of the secret service made rapid career progress. He offered the latest findings in research on the human body and knew how to keep it secret.[54]

The next steps in the use of chemicals in sport can be quickly summarized. They occurred gradually: an early decentralized phase, isolated large-scale secret experiments on cyclists or the Stasi Dynamo sports club, unstructured years of doping, numerous restructuring attempts and finally the conspiratorial State Research Plan 14.25 from 1974.[55] From then on it was possible to follow the logic of research on the human body in competition sport and to discover what the state sports project had to do with Interkosmos research. Did the state research in GDR sport establish a 'suitable ground model' in 1974, just as the monkey Tevton had been used as a model in space research?

State Research Plan 14.25 did not come out of the blue. 'Research projects in competition sport and the medical supervision of elite athletes must be closely linked,' a 1970 Stasi report stated.[56] Because of their 'instruments and apparatus' the country's military facilities – the main consultation centre of the Dynamo sports club, the Institute for Aerospace Medicine in Königsbrück, the main consultation centre of the Vorwärts army sports club in Frankfurt/Oder and the Central Institute for Sports Medicine in Kreischa – were regarded as being particularly suitable for this purpose.[57] A secret dossier in 1978 under the heading 'Development of new preparations' stated that the research projects would be carried out 'mainly through cooperation partners in departments of the Ministry of Science and Technology, the Academy of Sciences, the Ministry of Chemistry and the Ministry of Higher Education'.[58] It spoke of 'long-term cooperation'.[59] Sport was explicitly responsible for the practical implementation. More precisely: 'The results will be put into practice at the FKS.'[60] This meant that from the mid-1980s, space and sport were considered internally to be closely linked. Thus, the director of Technisch-Physikalischer Gerätebau Dresden wrote to the Academy of Sciences in connection with the problem of telemetry: 'We should like to consult with experts from your institute regarding the efficient sharing of development capabilities for use in space and competition sport research.'[61]

Military, Academy of Sciences and the research centres of GDR sport as a tight alliance. Knowledge of the maximum performance of trained bodies in sport was at all events useful for space. In 1983 'the number of classified research themes at the FKS requiring particular protection was increased from two to three'.[62] All three topics were connected with the ongoing Interkosmos research projects: (1) development of new performance-enhancing pharmaceutical substances; (2) training under hypoxic conditions; (3) latest image-measuring technique.[63] According to the files, important chemical breakthroughs were achieved in the GDR sports laboratory in 1983: the growth hormone somatropin, clomiphene, HCG and LHRH, and steroids not on the drug lists, various forms of blood doping, testatropin and epitestosterone.[64] A Stasi report states: 'All necessary steps are to be taken in 1983/84 for the use in the Olympic cycle 1984/88 of further steroids and steroid analogues, testosterone precursors and metabolites, neuropeptides and hormonal contraceptives as auxiliary substances in competition sport.'[65]

Of the 'thirty-five doping substances at least'[66] listed by the Central Investigation Department for Government and Reunification-Related Crime (ZERV) in its investigations after 1989, almost half were from the West. It was clearly evident that many a coercive research alliance had been formed in the course of East-West cooperation. For example, Prof. Dr. Michael Oettel, born in Jena in 1939, veterinarian and at the time research director of VEB GERMED in Dresden, asked a West German colleague at a conference on biochemical aspects of steroid research in Weimar in 1984: 'What possibilities are there for using antioestrogens to counter virilization in female athletes taking anabolics?'[67] The question was not acceptable. Oettel was required to retract it and reformulate it 'in a more general clinical manner'.[68]

This research discussion was able to take place as a matter of course in the mid-1980s because it had also become a matter of course in the carefully protected internal milieu. Standards were exchanged, business was conducted. The FKS also had regular contact with the West. For the research on hypoxia alone, it listed sixteen contact companies.[69]

Innovative value. The thing with alcohol. It trickled through the files in the 1980s like water. A Stasi report on track and field from this time states: 'Alcohol consumption has further increased, particularly among trainers, and with few exceptions they are becoming incapable of looking after the athletes.'[70] One trainer was apparently so far gone that he couldn't get rid of the Stasi: 'He was so drunk that he couldn't sign his release,' said the report.[71]

The thing with the girls. According to the questioning of the accused Manfred Höppner, the chief medical initiator of State Research Plan 14.25, children, particularly gymnasts, were also given chemicals as part of the 'Kaiser scheme', as it was called, or the osteochondrosis programme. Höppner kept a list of 218 minors who were given steroids on this basis.[72] The administration of Oral-Turinabol, the classic GDR anabolic, was justified as a treatment for Scheuermann's disease or osteonecrosis. The consequences for the girls: closed growth plates, massive growth impairment, chronic pain, a trauma forever. Girl swimmers were also ruthlessly exploited by the researchers. Strategic meetings were held in private. In the context of the major research on additional performance reserves, a Stasi officer reported that meetings were held in the apartment of the GDR swimming association doctor to discuss the strategy for the future use of auxiliary substances.[73] 'The discussion centred on the development and traceability of the depot injections of auxiliary substances in girls.'[74]

The thing with standards. The experiments, the tests, the programmes. Were they regulated by law in East Germany? A brief look at the legal documents shows clearly what the regulations covered. With regard to liability in experimental medicine, they say: 'Among the duties of the principal investigator ... is the acquisition of the subject or patient's consent. It should be obtained if possible in writing. . . . The selected persons are to be informed in detail about the experiment. Certain groups may not be used for specific examinations . . . even if they are available in principle for them: prison or reform school inmates, soldiers, mentally ill persons, women of child-bearing age, pregnant women and children.'[75]

The thing with the dual use. 'The classified state secret concerns the scientific study, testing and use of centrally managed and supervised auxiliary substances.'[76] From 1977 the FKS started to conclude 'service agreements with associations'.[77] From that time, not only 'operative application concepts' but also 'research concepts' were devised for active subjects.[78] In that connection: 'The work is to be carried out by the individual research groups in accordance with the written research concepts.'[79] From that time, athletes were thus studied both in the gym and in the laboratory. A dual use with research into chemicals and their application to enhance the New Body for the glorification of the state. In 1978 the research programme was refined once again. Apart from the master plan 'Additional performance reserves', there was now to be a concentration on 'certain selected associations' and on 'research findings with innovative value', that would give the country 'a head start in the international arena'.[80]

The archive in Freiburg contains the confidential research on sport that was decided and defended in Bad Saarow. 'Comparison of the effect of different anabolic steroids' with '221 active subjects'.[81] 'The influence on the drug metabolism of physical stress in rats and humans with and without the administration of steroid drugs', carried out on 'twenty-one competition athletes'.[82] The conclusion reads: 'The findings provide a basis for clinical trials of new drugs and for further examinations.'[83] Winfried Schäker's thesis on the neuropeptide oxytocin documented his research with seventy-eight subjects.[84]

Figures, figures, figures: '85 road-race cyclists, 112 long-distance runners, 18 boxers.'[85] 'Complex examinations of competition athletes (total subjects 221).'[86] 'Twelve subjects, three experimental groups, including former competition athletes.'[87] Without saying exactly how many subjects were involved, there was 'new research with ACTH molecules, like B17, the problem of beta-receptor blockers'.[88] Or: 'There were reports of examinations on the influence of ovulation inhibitors (the pill) on the performance of trained female competition athletes being carried out at the University Women's Clinic in Rostock.'[89] The research papers say of 'anabolic 12': 'We are the first to test it on humans, giving us a two-year lead.'[90] An intermediate FKS report says of tests with illegal research substances: 'As mentioned, a test plan for new substances was established in May. In consultation with the Institute for Pharmacology and the Secretary of the Central Expert Committee, the use of new substances (STS 646, STS 648, STS 482) will be tested on athletes.'[91]

The thing with the labels. Renaming, encoding, new designations, mock-ups. From May 1987, according to head doping physician Manfred Höppner, auxiliary substances were now to be called 'treatment measures'.[92] I stop short. Treatment measures? That says a lot. Words and their dimension. Sometimes the meaning takes time to sink in. But sometimes the words together as well. Not possible simply to rush ahead. As if the language no longer wanted to play along, just wanted to be left alone, had had enough. The following order came at nearly the same time: 'Apart from the trial subjects, the coding will be extended to trainers, doctors, officials and sports managers.'[93] Names were also to be replaced by codes in work plans, service agreements, research concepts and reports.[94] 'The auxiliary substances being used and tested are also to be coded. All auxiliary substance application concepts at the FKS are to be destroyed and new ones are not to be accepted.'[95] Everything had to be made unambiguous.

The thing with coding. There was one postdoctoral thesis that I put off reading every time I visited Freiburg. But now it

was time. It is the clinical epidemiological study by Hartmut
Riedel, born 1943, the doctor who was responsible for me from
28 September 1977 in Jena, first as a long jumper and then
as a sprinter.[96] This is what is written in my medical file.[97] In
Freiburg I read that he conducted his experiments between
1976 and 1983 and defended the thesis in Bad Saarow on 7 April
1987.[98] One of the supervisors was Hans Gürtler.

I leaf through Riedel's thesis: 'anthropometric parameters',
'pharmacotherapy'. The use of anabolic steroids is 'legitimate
and humane,' it says on page 10.[99] My eyes catch the phrase
'skinfold thickness'. My memory sticks there like a scratched
vinyl record. The grey Igelit stretcher in the Jena hospital ward,
the cold silver measuring appliances, the doctor's scrutinizing gaze. Me too, I think: '191 male and 174 female track and
field athletes in jumping disciplines'.[100] All coded. No name, no
background, just a number.

I continue browsing. Classical body fat measurement, I read,
is a method of determining the steroid level in the body. I
think again of Jacob. As a code, how can he be identified?
Like all the others? What to tell him? That I found myself in
the archive and still couldn't make any progress? That this
line of investigation leads to a dead-end? That the subjects are
not individuals but remain anonymous test objects? That the
coding cannot be traced back and history cannot be recon-
structed? That the researcher Hartmut Riedel has never said
a word about the fact that he conducted research on us? That
he was head of the research department in Kreischa from 1982
and was even the chief medical officer in charge of the track
and field athletes?[101] That he was thus a key figure in the GDR
sport drug programme? What can I say to Jacob? That Hartmut
Riedel was a doctor I wanted to like because he was calm, quiet,
worldly?

The aim of the experimental link is to study the influence of weightlessness on the geometry, development and stability of structures when microorganisms are linked with organic polymers. It is known that microorganisms interact with soluble polymer substances and that certain structures, known as 'flakes', can form.

Revolution of the apes

Contours. There was not just one single order that the research teams were required to agree to and carry out without question. It wasn't like that. So how was it? I look at the files and a pile of questions look back at me. What is legitimate research? How can any research be legitimate in a dictatorship? Is it about therapy or ideology? What does centralized control of research mean? What is system and what is an individual case? Who supervises everything? Who ensures transparency? Where are the tipping points, the limits? What about manipulation, secret service, deliberate hushing up? What is normal practice and at what point does research abandon its ethical coordinates and become a crime?[1]

Is the story of Interkosmos not just ultimately a story of encounters and interactions? There were orders, contracts, institutions, money, lots of political will. And from the researchers there were all kinds of ideas, power, career ambitions and greed. But isn't that always the case? Isn't the decisive criterion the fact that the researchers were practically all war children, that their driving force was winning and that the ideology, pressure, encounters and interactions made it possible for them to do so? And the research subjects? What about

Jacob, Astrid and the others? There are no simple answers. We need specific evidence.

The Interkosmos material consists of dossiers, concepts, contracts, research protocols, accounts, plans, corrections of plans. The material consists of words with the task of keeping the risk, the intrusion, the excesses out of the text. The language was meant to hide, cover up, make invisible, pretend something else, trivialize, filter out the reality, adapt the description to the utopia concept. Language as mask, as camouflage that turned the inherent lie into a reality. This doesn't make it easier to find the reality thirty or forty years ago in the material today.

October 2021. I'm standing next to the printer in Adlershof, in the library of the German Aerospace Centre, watching it print out and duplicate the past today, page after page. Sometimes the story falters, sometimes it gets stuck, sometimes it stops altogether. Then the efficient woman has to come. I am sweating. Some copiers are like ovens, I think. The more I copy, the warmer it gets. As if the paper was being baked.

I sort the pages, which are still warm. I want to arrange them by date, by subject, by research synapses. It's not easy. There is too much material; it is too disparate and only roughly sorted. The sources, the language, the thinking, the gaps. In one of the last minutes of the Scientific Council in Bad Saarow I read: 'To be destroyed: reports on results, suggested or non-processed topics, documents on the formal proceedings, correspondence with the Military Medicine Academy and the Faculty of Military Medicine, approval of theses, documents on doctoral courses, agendas, annual reports, profile lines.'[2]

Well, they didn't completely succeed. Not everything was destroyed. But what still exists and what has disappeared? What is history? What image do we pass on? I listen to the printer relentlessly spewing out pages. Did history simply overlook and forget the material in Adlershof? Could forgetting in this case mean hiding away and thus be just a piece of good fortune? But how far does this good fortune go? The pages keep coming. I recall the subdued tone of the dramatist Heiner Müller and his words about the tears at the frayed edges of history: 'It is what hurts and what disappears that is interesting.' But what is missing when something has disappeared? A portion of life, a piece of knowledge, the relationship to a time? How were the gaps to be talked about? How could the omissions be brought back? I look at the stacks of history on the left of the printer. Who, I ask myself, is Jacob in all this? The man in the room next to Sigmund Jähn, the national hero? A code in the Königsbrück experiments? A symbol? The anonymous person trying to locate his experience? Is he the unwanted chronicler of a system that decided that he shouldn't exist? Is his refusal to disappear today what secures him a place in history? Is that what I should tell him? Would it be any use to him?

Animal and human. Is that enough? While copying, I spot the year 1986, the first year of biomedicine in the Interkosmos project under the aegis of the Academy of Sciences. The driving force behind the research: settlement of space, mastery of the extraterrestrial universe. With the unanswered question as to what type of extreme body would be capable of doing this. A 'no longer organ-based body'? An 'environment-machine system'? Or the 'design of an electronic being'?[3] The concepts varied, the vanishing point of the sky remained the same. And the simultaneous experiments on the ground? I read: 'In implementation of the agreement reached during the joint consultation in October/November 1986, it was decided to conduct tests on the behaviour of substance P, endorphins, catecholamines and selected enzymes on sensory-deprived patients. In this experiment, the role of substance P was investigated for the first time in a model experiment with human subjects.'[4]

Model experiment with human subjects. Sensory-deprived patients. What was that about? An experiment protocol of

October 1984 states that 'twenty-five monkeys were again transported to Moscow from Sukhumi in preparation for further experiments'.[5] They were intended for 'preliminary work on the use of substance P for cosmonaut stress prevention'.[6] The required quantities of substance P were supplied by the East Berlin Institute for Substance Research (IWF), and the amounts were increased considerably from 1986 onwards.[7] Within Interkosmos, the IWF was the 'internal cooperation partner' in the context of two 'national state plans' relating to topics dealt with at Humboldt University and researched in the Department of Neuropathophysiology there. The titles: 'Physiological, biochemical and pharmacological processes in embryonal development and adults under terrestrial and space conditions' and 'Regulator peptides and sleep profile under conditions of long-term space travel.'[8]

As far as the research contracts were concerned, the Soviets seem to have appreciated the results provided by Karl Hecht and his team, because already in late 1986 the Soviet Ministry of Health and its Institute for Medicobiological Problems offered the researchers at Charité two lucrative new proposals: the joint establishment of a 'clinical complex' and a 'cell biology complex'.[9] A mega-project. The report states: 'The experts at the Institute for Medicobiological Problems (IMBP) would welcome it if additional laboratories at other universities or technical universities in the GDR could be included in the Charité–IMBP cooperation (e.g., Departments of Biology in Greifswald and Halle), but coordinated by Charité, as has functioned successfully in the case of Ilmenau Technical University.'[10]

Intensified cooperation between Moscow and Berlin, the establishment of a clinical and a cell biology complex, even more diversified contract research within the GDR, the interlinked experimental set-ups. That was the programme. In the protocol the addition: 'The partners agreed a blood sampling scheme to determine the neuropeptide dynamics in the blood (analogue to the 'sensory deprivation' experiment).'[11] And: 'The Soviet experts asked the GDR scientists to investigate the feasibility of creating . . . a digital memory to collect information on biorhythmic research conducted on humans and animals.'[12]

Research on humans and animals became more and more interlinked from 1986 onwards. The sources speak of 'logical continuation and development'.[13] The exclusive yardstick for the interaction was the required 'introduction into practical space medicine'.[14] In the plans for 1986 to 1990, Charité was now earmarked for six research projects.[15] The problem catalogue to be investigated sounded harmless at the time: 'cosmic chronobiology, chronomedicine and chronophysiology'.[16]

Undivided. And the research on 'sensory-deprived patients'? This was conducted primarily in connection with 'problems of cosmic biorhythmology'.[17] According to the reports, substance P was administered or various tests were carried out initially on 'five patients with primary dyssomnia', then '300 test subjects' and finally '120 persons (mentally ill and healthy)'.[18] 'In 1987 tests on a centrifuge were started on subjects with divergent health conditions,' it says in a report on gravitation research.[19] The next point: 'The interaction between cognitive processes, mental stress and substance P was examined on twenty-eight healthy patients. . . . Further tests are necessary before general conclusions can be drawn.'[20]

Research with substance P on patients in the Department of Neuropathophysiology at Charité became broader as the research projects grew in number. The tests looked at minute rhythms, individual stress resistance, sleep profiles, desynchronosis, activity profiles, hypergravitation, motion sickness. Research was carried out, for example, on '74 distance-learning students', 20 patients with sleep disorders, '180 subjects', '70 pregnant women', '200 nurses aged 17 to 19 years', '80 patients (40 alcoholics, 40 psychotics)'.[21] Sometimes simple stress tests were carried out; in many cases the research involved substance P. Pregnant women were also given Faustan (diazepam), 'which prevented mental stress'.[22]

And the ethical assessment of this research? On the one hand, it is quite clear, but at the same time it's difficult to grasp how it fitted in with the relativized morality of the GDR regime. As far as medical research ethics were concerned, all medicine was medicine for socialism, progress, peace and the wellbeing of the people – and thus a kind of collective ethics, principle ethics, victory ethics, arbitrary ethics, doing away with the individual's right to their own integrity.

A kind of authoritarian cloche, under which the individual and their moral right were miraculously absorbed by the collective. It was simply dispersed through the walls. Added to this was the blurring of boundaries through secrecy, the secret service, non-transparency, non-information. An approach that also equated the stories of the victims with those of the perpetrators. In the social narrative the victims were said to be non-existent. They were chosen to dissolve in some kind of apotheosis. The perpetrators were legitimized by the ideology and thus exonerated and hence also non-existent. In this way the regime removed injustice and crime from the ethical equation. A dispersal technique of a kind. As if milk were dribbled into water until the world was milky, in a state where no one was responsible for anything, then or later. It was the idea and vocabulary of a society that somehow developed a new natural order through these practices.

Bodily visions. In late November 1983 the Scientific Council in Bad Saarow accepted a postdoctoral thesis entitled 'Examinations of the performance of women aged 18 to 40 years under military conditions'.[23] Three weeks later Biosputnik 1514 was launched into space. It contained the two cosmonaut monkeys Abrek and Bion, but also a number of pregnant rats. Both the monkeys and the rats were essential features of the Interkosmos research and went through myriad versions, extensive testing and scenarios. But what did women in the military and expectant mothers in space have to do with one another?

It is interesting that in the 1980s women became a clear focus of research in the military and in the Interkosmos project. What did this mean? The Soviet programme for space research until the year 2000, which landed on the desks of the authorities at the Academy in East Berlin in the mid-1980s, explicitly indicated that a body that was getting ready to leave the Earth's atmosphere had to be seen as existing in a completely new dimension.[24] The research was looking at 'the development of future spaceships' and hence flights lasting 'considerably longer than two years'.[25] What kind of New Man did they think would be conquering space in twenty or thirty years' time? Male cosmonauts was one thing, but who would guarantee life up there in this infinitely inhospitable universe? How would the species survive? How was the universe to be tamed if the cosmonauts died before their destination was even in sight? How was life to be organized so that it could exist weightlessly, in a hypergravitational situation, over a long period?

The secret postdoctoral thesis had its title changed to 'The performance of women and their suitability for military use' and was defended in Bad Saarow on 9 September 1988. The introduction stated: 'In the history of military activity, the recruitment of women in the army has become a characteristic of modern warfare. . . . Just as they can replace men in civilian jobs, they can do so to a large extent in the military as well. . . . This is a logical consequence of the equality of opportunity that has already been achieved in all other areas of social life in the GDR.'[26]

An official model GDR woman? Was there such a thing? I think of the women workers represented on outsize bronze statues in front of schools, in parks and squares. Oddly compact and actually unrealistic bodies. An A shape, a mythical body. Sturdy, striding, resolute, armoured. The ideal image of a progressive East German woman: full-time worker, typically with two children, socially active, running the home, multitasking and, of course, uncomplaining. The female body in the military as 'characteristic of modern warfare'? It was above all a construct designed by male war children switching between two dictatorial visions of womankind. Leni Riefenstahl's film of the 1936 Berlin Olympic Games showed a muscular, radiant male body created from several servile women's bodies. The three women burn in the flames before the warrior opens his eyes and with the torch of victory in his hand runs into the light of the glorious, newly built stadium. This ideal of the life-giving child-bearing woman in Nazism can be contrasted with the working Soviet mother needed above all as builder of socialism. By means of a multiple and highly ambivalent process, she was not only sacrificed but also above all virilized.

The modern body war referred to in the postdoctoral thesis could thus be the blending of these two body ideals to create the New Space Woman. The Soviet version of the manipulation of the female body – basically a purpose-built worker model – merges with the Nazi dedicated child-bearing version. Together they formed the East German ideal of a robust androgenized female body, improved and performing efficiently and above all as a child-bearing model, leading mankind under extreme conditions to the promised land in space. That was the idea, at least, but how did it work in practice?

Mother-offspring system. After Biosputnik 1514 returned to Earth, research on the mother-offspring system became a focus within space medicine.[27] It was particularly interested in the specific relationship between reproduction and chronic stress, in other words weightlessness. One report states: 'It is known that chronic stress can considerably impair reproductive capability.'[28] A number of tests ensued in which pregnant female rats were given substance P. The conclusions: 'An important finding of these tests is that hypergravitation and substance P have different effects at different stages of pregnancy. Under hypergravitational conditions, protection of the mother's organism takes precedence over that of the child's. Comparative tests reveal that the pregnant female organism is much more resistant to hypergravitation than the male organism.'[29]

The fact that the mother's survival instinct was stronger than her willingness to protect her young must have been quite a blow for the researchers conducting the extra-atmospheric space project. A significant and fundamental finding in relation to the project as a whole. It meant that the willingness of women to sacrifice themselves had limits. Obviously a survival instinct. Perhaps the miracle of life? But how to ensure the species reproduced beyond Mars? And what about the second finding, that pregnant women in space were more resistant than male cosmonauts? How was this to be dealt with? The simplest way was to continue the dedicated project: research, research and more research. A follow-up protocol states: 'The biomaterial (plasma, adrenal glands, hypothalami, foetuses, placentas) obtained from the IMBP (Moscow) was examined to determine stress-induced changes (hypergravitation) and the influence on them of substance P.'[30] A central question remained: 'How do stress and substance P influence the foetus and placenta test parameters?'[31]

Placenta and foetus research was also discussed by the scientists in Bad Saarow. From 1986 two major research projects, numbers 13 and 14, were mentioned in particular. The minutes of the meeting of 5 September 1986: 'The rector conference decrees that the focus should be on creating closer links between science and production. Performance data are to be studied critically at the highest international level.'[32] The next agenda item at this meeting was the examination of the post-doctoral thesis of Hartmut Riedel, my former doctor. Then the meeting discussed the thesis: 'The prisoner in the role of patient – investigation of doctor-patient relationship in prison hospitals in the GDR'.[33] Finally the meeting considered the start of central research projects 13 and 14.[34] 'Design and discussion of research concept "patient with diminished immune response". Since June 1986 clinical trial "Selective decontamination in immune-compromised patients". Maintenance of cooperation with the clinical gnotobiology working group at the Wilhelm Pieck University of Rostock. Decision to be made on cooperation in the special research and planned state projects on clinical gnotobiology.'[35] Gnotobiology, the germ-free breeding of animals for immunology, was a global research phenomenon at this time.

It all sounded like a lot of technical mumbo-jumbo, but in the Interkosmos system it was anything but. The two research themes were dealing with the long-term New Man in Space, where immunology and reproduction were important factors. Project 13 was devoted to 'performance-oriented uses of women'. The protocols here were shorter and only the term 'placenta research' is mentioned.[36] One of the follow-up protocols in Bad Saarow in 1987 contains the conclusion: 'In view of the experience regarding risky research, the involvement of a wider range of potential beneficiaries (partners) should be considered. This could apply to both Interkosmos and to users of ionizing radiation in the GDR. The issue should be brought up in the Medical Science Council so as to prepare for possible long-term inclusion in a state programme.'[37]

Risky research. Involvement of potential beneficiaries. Military research increasingly shifted its grey areas, depths, limitless borders to the civilian sphere, a fact that is barely mentioned in the Bad Saarow records, in contrast to Adlershof. The files seem to be thinned out and the traces increasingly hard to follow. This could have to do with the systematic destruction of files at the latest from 1991 onwards. It is also possible that there are still undiscovered records with potential partners.

The factual situation is unclear, the research framework vague. My small archive exegesis on biomedicine, military and Interkosmos will be based explicitly on what can be documented. Research is in the early stages, that's all. An initial view of a dark area, a set of questions on a mass of unsorted material that needs to be further clarified.

Wuhan. The 8th Symposium of the International Academy of Cosmonautics took place in October 1989 in Tashkent. The agenda included the findings from 'manned space flights, biosatellites, simulated space flights on Earth . . . and the programmes for future space flights'.[38] The usual issues were discussed: hormones, microbiology and genetics, vestibular functions, bone septa, animal models and life-support systems.[39] Karl Hecht reported on the margins that 'a group of young scientists from the FRG, notably from the Aerospace Medicine Institute and the Sports Medicine Institute, both in Cologne', had asked to visit his institute on 28 October 1989.[40] The report continued: 'A psychophysiological working group in the CSSR showed a video film about the "tunnel" experiment (three-week bunker experiment in complete isolation)'. Hecht also commented: 'The West was very interested in taking part in experiments in Soviet spacecraft. All these countries were negotiating on the margins of the symposium with Glavkosmos' – the main space authority in the Soviet era for cooperation and commercial exploitation with other countries.[41]

The fateful date 9 November 1989 seemed to be coming closer and closer. As if the revolution was also intruding into the documented history. As if even those affairs that had been filed away were becoming restless. The reports and protocols increasingly contained references to the mood on the streets and above all showed a discernible nervousness. What was going to happen? Crime was on the rise in Tashkent, it was said. The attempt to protect confidentiality at the Leipzig FKS was failing. Demonstrations were being held regularly in Berlin in front of the research institute windows. The only place where everything was still apparently running smoothly was on the lake in Bad Saarow, where the staff sought to continue to conduct research and hold on to the long-standing daily routine. Among the various topics under study, immunology became increasingly prominent in the last two or three years of the Interkosmos complex.

I might have overlooked the question of immunology in the haystack of documents, but suddenly it emerged in autumn 2021. This was due solely to one particular detail and with the here and now. I found a memo in one of the documents: 'Visit to Beijing, Wuhan, 18 April to 5 July 1988'.[42] The Institute of Virology in Wuhan had been founded in 1956 and has had its present name since 1978. So it is an institution with a long tradition. Since it was visited in summer 1988 by East German Interkosmos experts, it may be assumed that the Chinese were also interested in the space project.

The interest in virus research at Interkosmos was directly linked with the space vision from 1986 onwards: the New Man in a completely new dimension. Extract from a draft paper: 'In contemplating future interplanetary flights it should be borne in mind that there are considerable differences in comparison with long-term orbital flights, where there are many con-nections with Earth that would not exist with interplanetary flights.'[43] The aim was to study 'the influence of cosmic factors during long-term flights in orbit and on a flight to Mars'.[44]

All biomedicine, now called life sciences, all research in space could only confirm the implosion of the body during long-term flights. Not only muscles, not only blood, not only bones, eyes, heart – but also the immune system had to face up to the problems of weightlessness, radiation and the grow-ing tediousness and general discomfort of the human body the longer the flight lasted and the farther from Earth. So much for the research. What next? One of the consultations in 1986 of the permanent working group on cosmic medicine had two main virus research issues on the agenda: 'gene expression and activation of endogenous virus genomes in cell cultures under space conditions' and 'immunological reaction of the human organism under real and simulated weightlessness conditions'.[45]

After that time, immunology was a permanent feature of the research portfolio. An immunology working group was established in Bad Saarow, although there was already an immunology institute. The management protocol in May 1987 stated: '"Clinical gnotobiology" international symposium in Rostock in October 1987. GDR research three years ahead of Japan. Meetings in Tokyo, Essen, Warsaw. The immunology working group requests research on academic works on clinical gnotobiology currently being undertaken above all in the FRG'.[46] The protocol of June 1987 also states that the medical service of the National People's Army should investigate 'immunological problems in long-term space travel'.[47]

Research focused on new antiviral substances and resistance to viral infections. It appeared that without intensified virus research, the New Man would not achieve the desired aim.

Aversive. I am sitting in front of my computer and staring at a blank screen. What should I write? It's October 2021. Investigation of the charge by the Stasi records authority of 'violation of confidentiality and special duty to confidentiality' has been abandoned by the public prosecutor's office in Berlin.[48] 'It has not been possible to identify a perpetrator,' it says in the grounds.[49] The letter indicates that no investigation took place and only one person was questioned.

Gerd Machalett continues to write his articles. The next one appeared in *Rubikon* on 4 August 2021 with the title 'The fake scandal'.[50] In it he attacked the makers of an ARD documentary and the main subject in the film, a former sprinter, who had apparently been the object of a research consortium that Machalett had once been a member of. The 'bloated lies', the 'myth of forced doping', the 'processing industry', I read. In the film I see a man walking through an East German town. He says his piece at length. He shows his diaries, he has lots of documents. There can be no doubt that this documentary is significant. The man was seriously damaged through no fault of his own and needs help. It makes no difference. He is publicly pilloried.

'Where one looks, speaks and writes influences what one sees and how one formulates traumas,' writes José Brunner.[51] I stop at the concept of collective perpetrator trauma that occurs frequently in Brunner's books. What about Machalett and the others? What about the long history of dictatorship in East Germany and the continuing taboos regarding responsibility? What about the spatial component of trauma, as Brunner writes? Perhaps it is some kind of being. Perhaps it occurs, like the victim trauma, in a specific place and can never be dissociated from it. I imagine that the collective perpetrator trauma is an aversion. That it continuously scans the surface of a society to determine whether it is becoming a subject of interest. That it has a delicate stomach, a weak heart and lots of twitchy nerves. I try to imagine how the collective perpetrator trauma felt in November 1989. Whether people called or met each other to agree on how to deal with the new situation. I imagine that it waited first of all. Who knows what will happen? In fact, not a lot, at least for the collective perpetrator trauma. I imagine that at some point it understood this. That it already knew a lot, even what had been going on before it became a collective perpetrator trauma. For example, what was planned, who planned it, what the atmosphere was like at the meetings where decisions were made on the test subjects. To that extent, the collective perpetrator trauma is by its nature well ahead of an awareness of the victim trauma.

I would like to tell José Brunner that it's about spatiality but also about time. About the preparations at the time, about the knowledge at the time, about the actions at the time, about the time in our heads. I try to imagine what preparations and follow-up mean in connection with a trauma, with the internal narrative structure. Where victims and perpetrators part ways, where they are completely unconnected, where there is no communication. Two competing experiences. An inalterability that cannot be explained away. Something quite disconnected. Unless it's possible to find a point of transition, a *rite de passage*, a politico-cultural script that gives this experience a different status.

The years after 1989 and how the collective perpetrator trauma learned to use the advantages of a society that it had fought against until 1989. The subtexts, the ignored facts, the reorganization through which the status of victims remained fragile. Who was allowed to identify themselves as a victim? Shouldn't the victim have to produce a clear linear narrative? The collective perpetrator trauma that began first to aim its offensive in particular at victims: 'imposters', 'liars', 'slanderers', 'traitors'. They have to be got rid of, they're in the way, they need to be kept down. Campaigns are deliberately designed to confuse and blur the issue.

I imagine that the unknown soldier is quite simply the collective perpetrator trauma, in whose shadows all kinds of characters can emerge, like the woods in Shakespeare. They are there, there are lots of them, they live out their aversions, they sit at their computers and put together their attacks, they wait until it's dark. Then the pamphlets are sent to ministries, authorities, media, foundations, preferably to all of them. My attempts to defend myself fall on deaf ears under the pretext of freedom of speech. Historical facts? No longer relevant. Does it have to be taken seriously? At all events, the attacks have extensively put an end to the political project regarding GDR sports victims.

Abkhazia. The Sukhumi monkeys used in the 1920s in the first cross-breeding experiments, launched into space like

Abrek and Bion in 1983 and later exploited for the latest virus research. I come across a newspaper article about the Georgian idyll, the Black Sea, long palm beaches, huge white magnolias, olives, laurel and the monkey nursery on Mount Trapeze above Sukhumi. I read in Irena Josifovna Volk's book written in 1973: 'The monkeys here are very useful. They are well fed and looked after and account is taken of their special characteristics.'[52]

1989, 1991, 1993. The Soviet Union imploded like the New Man in Space. A question of statics? No one was left in Sukhumi to look after the monkeys. The country was busy with other things. But there were lots of monkeys. More than a thousand, I read. The huge space project was no longer relevant. No money left. Even when the cosmonaut Alexander Lasutkin on Soyuz TM-25 should have been brought back in 1997 because of the numerous technical problems, he remained up there. There were no funds to bring him back. So he carried on flying until the irreversible muscular atrophy.[53]

I know too little about rhesus monkeys who spend their whole lives in cages. But they must have felt something in 1989. That something was different. Perhaps they had an inkling of what was going on, or perhaps they were just hungry. Perhaps they heard the mating calls of their colleagues set free in the wild for research purposes. Whatever the case, they opened their enclosures, gathered at the entrance to the farm, set off through the forest and down to the city. To hear the sea for the first time. To sniff and rub up against each other for the first time. To squat on the lakeside promenade lined with palm trees for the first time. To search for their own food for the first time, at least what they really wanted. To wander through the town for the first time. Perhaps they knew that something different was coming, a new era. It didn't matter. It happened. A revolution of the apes.

In all discussions it was emphasized that many situations in space flight can be simulated on the ground. Only the long-lasting weightlessness cannot be simulated on Earth.

Zentrales Archiv des Deutschen Zentrums für Luft- und Raumfahrt e.V., Göttingen, BAAR, A850, unnumbered.

Back to the future

Turnarounds. 9 November 1989 as the happiest moment in German history? It was, unquestionably. But how did the days and weeks following the historic miracle feel for those whose power was slipping away from them? From the notes made by an employee of Stasi department XVIII on 17 November: 'Very complicated situation . . . MfS no longer exists . . . safeguard IM network, carry a weapon'; 22 November: 'Essential to secure all funds'; 24 November: 'Department XVIII/8 preparing for transfer, clear out safes!!!'; 25 November: 'On the cadre question: all securely tied up, everyone will be safely reallocated. Warning: don't speak about social security, sums paid outside the organ'; 5 December: 'Secure objects, additional blocking . . . consultation with general: carrying a weapon recommended, prepare narratives by 20 December 1989, department XVII to continue working for now in present structures! Policy for change not arrived at quickly enough'.[1]

Yet again a place where words need space. Where they say stop so that they can be looked at and understood. *Continue working in present structures.* A thought that opens up like a fan to explore the future story in depth and announces what it has found on the way. The old transforming into the new.

Policy for change. The turnaround. I see a swimmer reaching the end of the pool and preparing to turn around. A gymnast doing the most daring turns on the uneven bars. Autumn 1989 and the policy for change with its filigree language codes, the information fog in the new, now unlimited fields of operation. The last breaths of the dictatorship, the historical looping of the perpetrators. The 'realistic abrogation of reality,' as Hannah Arendt described the process.

There is too much material, too much history. I want to stay on track and piece the puzzle together. 'The object to be kept in the archive can be understood only if its origins are known,' writes the archivist Erdmut Wizisla.[2] The origins, East Germany, understanding, lifting of files. Every archive no doubt harbours questions. We know that from our personal archive of feelings. But it also applies to public archives. They also have their gaps; they also consist of fragmentary knowledge. Who seeks, who organizes, who presents the narrative? And how to manage without archives, like knowledge magazines, without stable counter-memories as signposts, guides, possible correctives?

Implants. Am I finished here? I leaf through the papers one more time. What has been omitted in the documentation about Interkosmos and biomedicine? What has been left out? Research on children, for example. For the military, children were an ongoing research issue. In that regard, ideas for theses cropped up regularly at meetings in Bad Saarow. Already in 1975 experiments involving schoolchildren took place as part of state planning project 6.01.00, 'Increasing learning potential'. They came under the Ministry of Science and Technology and were the responsibility of the Ministry of Public Education and the Academy of Sciences of the GDR.[3] Other research themes were added in the 1980s: 'Changes in obstetrics following the introduction of electronic birth monitoring: a comparative study of patients at the Charité University Women's Hospital and the Central Military Hospital Gynaecology Clinic',[4] 'Diagnostic urine sampling via 600 suprapubic bladder punctures of children of various ages',[5] 'Physical and performance development of child swimmers aged 7 to 9 years'.[6] All of these theses were defended in Bad Saarow. After 1986 this complex research field was mentioned in the protocols only under a simple heading. When a framework agreement on cardiovascular diagnosis was concluded in late 1986, the word 'paediatric clinic' was mentioned in the protocols in connection with the Academy of Sciences, the Central Institute for Cardiovascular Research, the MMA Medical Clinic and the Institute for Nuclear Medicine.[7] No indication of the place or further details, as if any information would have been too much information.

What else? The research at the Academy of Sciences of the GDR with the Stasi under the cover of the military, for example. Following *zwo sechsundzwanzig*, the Sigmund Jähn speech project, a speech analysis device was to be developed as part of the 1982 Interkosmos programme to help understand the psycho-emotional state of the cosmonauts.[8] A project which also attracted the keen interest of the GDR secret service, as it would enable it to carry out speech or noise analyses of regime opponents it was monitoring. And also, the new technology would make it possible to listen and wiretap with greater accuracy and focus. The term 'correlation measuring station' was suggested as a suitable cover name.[9] A documented record indicates that the project was part of the 'special budget item' and 'implemented on behalf of the Institute for Language Research and the Ministry of State Security in the Centre for Technical Apparatus Engineering in Berlin-Adlershof'.[10] A subsequent meeting emphasized the 'multivalent applications' of the device, coordinated the 'collaboration with the Soviet partner' and confirmed the framework for an 'economic agreement' to be signed, at the insistence of those involved, only by the Academy of Sciences and the Ministry of National

Defence.[11] The protocol states succinctly: 'The interests of the Ministry of State Security will be allowed for in the agreement and supported by an agreement with the Ministry of National Defence.'[12]

What else? The research on cosmic pharmacology, for example. A term that appeared increasingly in the Interkosmos protocols during the 1980s, providing indication of a reality that had to do with the precariousness of the space mechanism, which became increasingly visible as the years went by: the longer and farther the flights, the more inevitable the collateral damage to bodies. If the Soviets wished to continue their interplanetary objective – which they did at any cost – this would involve a considerable amount of additional research and a clear path towards a New Man created through complex chemical substances. East German focuses in that context were: 'Investigation of pharmacological substances for prevention of motion sickness',[13] 'Investigation of anti-stress effect of sequences of substance P',[14] 'Dynamics of biorhythms, stress, chronotherapy, chronopharmacology',[15] 'Potential for pharmacological correction of weightlessness in bone tissue'.[16] My eyes dwelled on a few half-sentences from the 1980s: 'massive changes in jaw and dental roots',[17] 'lymphocyte cultures',[18] 'mechanics of respiration and blood gases',[19] 'cell repairs'.[20]

The humans in space and those on the ground. Plus Bion, Abrek, the pregnant rats. And the many others. A dynamic that is not meant to appear in any picture, as if it doesn't belong to any time. Blood gases, dental roots, jaws. These research creatures are permanently orbiting around us. That they are there, squatting, waiting, looking after themselves, starving, freezing, while in the meantime their cells are being repaired or other things are being done to them. I have again to pay attention to what these words are doing here. That they remain on track and keep going. The omnipresence of space and the weightlessness in the bone tissue. That was not only research into the extreme but also science going deep into the body. And again and again countless references to related research projects: 'Influence of weightlessness on differentiation processes as illustrated by the bone marrow',[21] 'Acceleration and altitude physiology research',[22] 'Determination of the pain threshold in humans',[23] 'Elimination of stress damage in humans',[24] 'Experiments on bacteria and virus genetics'.[25]

Last but not least, the constant extension of the monkey research, as it was called in the archives. It is mentioned in the Interkosmos documents from 1982: 'For that purpose, electrodes were implanted in the brain structures controlling blood circulation and relevant to emotions of three rhesus monkeys.'[26] The operations were complicated: 'A further operation on 28 October 1982 (addition of further capacitors to the implanted system) did not produce the desired result because of the difficult insulation situation. For that reason, a further system with cast capacitors will be implanted and tested in the second half of December 1982.'[27] The conclusion: 'The animals appear suited for examinations to demonstrate the influence of psychosocial stress on the brain, as an active structure for analysis of the resultant diverse disruptions to the central nervous system.'[28]

Research that was evidently carried out in East Berlin. Where precisely? At all events, future plans were made with it. The issue was still the 'guarantee of psychological reliability of the crews of long-term space missions,' as it stated in a work protocol of the cosmic psychology section.[29] The plans for 1989 were as follows: 'Preparation and implementation of joint physiological examinations on higher nerve activity and oxygen tension in the brain of primates during the flight of a biosatellite in 1989'.[30]

Decommissions. On 1 September 1990, the Military Medicine Academy in Bad Saarow lost its status as an institute of higher education. It was removed from the register of such institutes and was no longer able to issue a *facultas docendi*.[31] The

Academy was instructed to close down by the end of 1990. It continued to operate thereafter as a clinic under civilian management.[32] A clear break – but not in the minds of the military researchers there. In 2015, a quarter century after the Academy had been decommissioned, its last director, Helmut Reichelt published the first and to date only study of the institution, in which he stated that all public criticism was invalid. Top secret military research? – Belonged to the cabinet of curiosities.[33] Complete confidentiality? – 'It prevented the findings of the GDR researchers and of military medicine from being known and recognized.'[34] Order to destroy the files in 1990? – Not mentioned at all. Instead, Reichelt wrote: 'When in 1990, on the day after the dissolution of the National People's Army and the integration of all material in the Bundeswehr, groups from military and civilian committees turned up with orders to confiscate and inspect all confidential documents from the Military Medicine Academy, they were extremely disappointed and frustrated that there was no trace of anything they had confidently expected to find.'[35]

The author responded in detail to just two criticisms. On the subject of research into chemical and biological weapons, he wrote: 'This did not exist, nor were the conditions (poison laboratories) available for working with such dangerous substances.'[36] He failed to mention the Military Technical Institute in Königs Wusterhausen, just 40 kilometres from Bad Saarow, since the mid-1970s the main site for military biological warfare research.[37] And the other criticism? 'The head of the Military Medicine Academy also felt obliged to refute the claim by Western researchers that doping substances were developed and tested on humans there,' wrote Helmut Reichelt, referring to himself. 'Tests were carried out in the Medical Clinic and Institute for Immunology as to whether improved performance as a result of training could be measured through biochemical methods, but no performance-enhancing drugs or psychopharmaceuticals were used.'[38]

Gosen bunker. The change of system was much more professional at the Academy of Science Institute for Space Research, no doubt because of the particular interest of the Federal Republic in this leading institute. 'The need for a strong partner to continue the work was recognized there more quickly than in other academic establishments.'[39] This could only have been referring to the German Aerospace Centre (DLR). And this was indeed the case. 'The evaluation of the different areas began in October 1990 and the assessment by the Scientific Council was presented in March 1991. This assessment of the Institute was also positive.'[40] Agreement was quickly reached. No doubt also because of the need to 'continue developing aerospace medicine in the Federal Republic'.[41] At all events 'the research areas of the Institute for Space Research [were integrated] in the DLR' from 1 January 1992.[42]

Was there a zero hour when it came to scientific research? What was the situation with the national responsibility of the Academy during the dissolution of the GDR? What became of the research elites during the historical interregnum? The source material does not mention anything untoward after the change in 1989 and suggests that business continued as usual. Because there was safety in holding onto things that could continue simply at this time of global upheaval? Like the 'Interkosmos programme', like the 'bilateral agreement between Charité and the Institute for Medicobiological Problems in Moscow', like the 'permanent working group on cosmic biology and medicine of the participating countries'.[43]

December 1990: Specialists from Moscow and Berlin met at the Charité to discuss prospective research projects. The studies under conditions of long-term isolation were to be continued.[44] There was also discussion on 'results in the area of psychopharmacology and psychoneurology'.[45] The experts met almost every month in an atmosphere of extreme tension. The East German researchers wanted to be sure they landed safely in the new world. In April 1991 they informed their colleagues in Moscow that they had submitted 'five scientific projects' to the DARA, the German Space Agency, founded in Bonn in 1989.[46] Attached to the protocol was a long list of subjects for 'interinstitutional research'. Once again it was about the Medilab space laboratory, substance P, chronostatus, isolation, monkeys in extreme situations and hypomagnetic fields.[47] In addition, a new 'agreement on scientific and technical cooperation' for the period 1991 to 1995 between Berlin and Moscow on the problem of the 'influence of extreme environmental factors on the functional states of humans and animals' was presented.[48]

On 26 April 1991, barely two weeks after the meeting in Moscow, the agreements were put into practice, because on this day there was a visit to the Gosen site to examine 'the creation of a future training research centre for space medicine and physiological questions'.[49] In the GDR days, the bunker in Gosen had served the secret service as an 'alternative leadership post'. A Stasi atomic bunker, so well-equipped that spy boss Markus Wolf could have continued to control his network of agents in the West even in the case of a nuclear attack. Under the new situation, the idea was mooted of using the Gosen bunker for the latest now pan-German aerospace medicine. Who had this idea? How did the Charité research team know about the secret service site? Who arranged it all?

On 14 June 1991, Karl Hecht, still head of the Institute for Pathological Physiology, wrote to the rector of Humboldt University in Berlin: 'Your Excellency, allow me to inform you about some activities and facts regarding the continuation and development of aerospace medicine research by our Institute.'[50] He wrote about Medilab, whose start-up had been postponed until 1996, about chronostatus, kinetosis and substance P regulation, crew simulations and the Gosen isolation study project.[51] He mentioned the amount of 23 million marks for research funding.[52] He concluded: 'Excellency, I would like to draw your attention to these projects because I believe that our university would be ideally suited to carry them out and that they would demonstrate our excellent scientific quality. At the same time, I would ask you to support us in the use of the atomic bunker and some of the premises in Gosen, which are required for the implementation of the above-mentioned projects.'[53]

As a next step, Hecht suggested a project to consolidate what was to happen in the Gosen bunker: 'For the selection of astronauts and also to monitor their health, performance and wellbeing, planned long-term travel to other planets, e.g., Mars, a set of experiments is required that would demonstrate the dynamics of complex modes of behaviour.'[54] In an additional paper he stated: 'In preparing for future national and international missions (Columbus, Eureka, Spacelab, MIR), previous crew simulation studies as a form of basic research should be intensified and expanded. The main aims are chronopsychophysiological and chronobiological experiments with crew *simulations* under extreme conditions in the period 1991 to 1998.'[55]

Behind these words was the idea of the Gosen bunker as a genuine future space for long-term research to investigate everything there was to be known about 'human behaviour patterns' in isolation.[56] It was suggested that subjects remain up to eighteen months in the bunker. According to the proposal, the bunker crew would consist of the following: 'Six male test subjects; interdisciplinary expertise: (1) doctor with knowledge of psychophysiology, (2) biologist with knowledge of biochemistry, (3) psychologist with knowledge of individual and social psychology, (4) technician (electronics engineer), (5) mathematician, (6) journalist.'[57]

Different terrains. The layers of time. The history of sources. The facts, traces, clues, documents, gaps. My search is at an end. After 1992 there are no more documents from Adlershof. It is unlikely that the six-man crew was operational in Gosen.

But there are lots of bunkers, lots of relabelling, lots of tacit agreements, lots of sky. The academies, the scientific councils, the integrative cooperations, the researchers and the coded research material, the damage situation, the continuous instrumentalization, the monitoring creatures. It's time to visit Jacob. What he wants to know remains encrypted. There is no simple answer and, above all, no happy ending. But I can tell him what his place was like.

It is December 2021. I get into my car and set off eastwards to a small town in Brandenburg near the Polish border. I switch on the radio. There is a report about the German astronaut Matthias Maurer, who set off on 11 October 2021 on a six-month ISS mission. The Australian aerospace expert Morris Jones has just said: 'The moon is a large place with different terrains.' I think of the stars in the sky and those that land in the waiting rooms of history. Whose bodies often enough become part of a new time reckoning. So new that they no longer recognize their old lives.

East Germany, which we think we know. But it is always different. Even wilder and bleaker. Even further and harder. Even more physical and incomprehensible. I find Jacob's street. The usual apartment blocks. I find his nameplate and ring. Nothing. I have a smoke and ring again. A man walks along the empty street, heads for the building where I'm standing, looks at me briefly, opens the door. 'Are you looking for someone?' he asks. The situations, the faces, the words. As if I'm in a film that started without me. My head is full of stuff. I ask about Jacob. The man and I stand in front of the door and look at one another. In the glances, this pause that collapses on itself as if it was scratching away the last protective skin. He shakes his head. No idea. He's somehow disappeared. I haven't seen him for a long time.

Space force. I drive back to Berlin on the country roads, through the Brandenburg villages with their light brick churches that glow in December like sunspots. I like the pines, the sand, the big sky. The summers on the Brandenburg lakes that represent all summers, in the past and in the future and the ones we will never see. Summer is summer, but these here are particularly happy. I drive through the countryside with the feeling that I've lost something. Where is Jacob?

The planned manoeuvres in space, the 'weightlessness model', the 'no longer organ-based body'. Concepts from the cybernetic culture of the Cold War. They are by no means obsolete: in the past ten years the conquest of extraterrestrial space has experienced a remarkable renaissance. Stellar power equals global power? In February 2019 US President Donald Trump declared space to be a 'new war front' and signed a decree establishing an independent space force. The sky has become a new theatre for global political realignment. As a power market and a money market.

For example, the Mars One project launched in 2011 by a private Dutch foundation. A one-way mission to Mars was announced on the Internet. The plan was to colonize the Red Planet. According to the Mars One founders, the first humans – two women and two men – would live in a permanent settlement on Mars by 2023. In recruiting for their mission, the organizers of the great flight from Earth betted cleverly that there were enough Mars freaks around, and they were right on the money. Within three years, 220,000 visionaries from 140 countries had volunteered and paid for their final journey. Within five years, the Mars colonizing website had been seen by 20 million users. Mars One Ventures AG in Basel, which was responsible for the financing and marketing, was even traded for a time on the Frankfurt stock exchange and earned over a billion dollars. The money also flowed because the spectacular trip had been designed from the outset as a gigantic reality show. The Dutch TV production company Endemol was to turn the entire project into the 'greatest media event in the history of the world'. The preparations were in

full swing, despite the absence of any technical, economic or
ethical expertise. The end was inevitable. In January 2019 Mars
One filed for bankruptcy. All of the money was gone. The fas-
cination of thousands of Mars enthusiasts ended in a nebulous
fake mission.

I pass Grünheide and think about all my walks with the
writer Joachim Walther at the lake, about our archive of banned
literature in East Germany, about Jürgen Fuchs, who lived for
a while nearby, about the imprint of the past in the present.
About a landscape with time loops that look like spirals, and
of course about Elon Musk, who is building his giga-factory in
Grünheide. According to his own publicity, it will be 'the most
progressive electric vehicle production line in the world'. The
cameras, his smile, the perfect marketing. Elon Musk as head of
the e-vehicle maker Tesla and the Californian space company
SpaceX, as chairman of the board of administrators of the solar
energy company Solar City and co-owner of the neurotechnol-
ogy company Neuralink. As someone who is approaching his
expansive excursions into space more precisely or at least with
greater determination than the people from Mars One. On
31 May 2012, his Space X spacecraft *Dragon* returned safely to
Earth. After Sputnik, the Cold War and the Space Shuttle, it
was the first successful mission by a privately developed rocket
and space capsule. It was hailed in the media as an advance, a
breakthrough, a new space era.

'Space X sends a rocket up about once a month, carrying satellites for companies and nations and supplies to the
International Space Station.'[58] The advantage of the Musk
method is that it is made entirely in the USA and can thus dis-
engage from the exorbitantly expensive Russian space branch.
'The retirement of the space shuttle made the United States
totally dependent on the Russians to get astronauts to the ISS.
Russia gets to charge $70 million per person for a trip and to
cut the United States off as it sees fit during political rifts,'
writes the Musk biographer Ashlee Vance.[59] He continues:

'With Space X, Musk is battling the giants of the US military-industrial complex, including Lockheed Martin and Boeing. He's also battling nations – most notably Russia and China.'[60]

Whatever the case, opinions are divided about the giga-man Musk. For some he is the Leonardo da Vinci of the twenty-first century, an uncompromising visionary, a one-man venture capital company, who is not only willing to take extreme risks but also makes highly complex physical products, a 'general marshalling troops to secure victory'. For others he is someone who sells false hopes, 'a sci-fi version of P.T. Barnum who has gotten extraordinarily rich by preying on people's fear and self-hatred'.[61] Whatever people think of this tech rock star, he is constantly connected with the future, with the attempt 'to do the impossible on top of the impossible'.[62]

Transport problems. I approach Berlin. The words want to touch down, to reach solid ground, like Dragon capsules. I think of the slurry of history, of what we call progress, the joy, the consequences, the price. What we can no longer get rid of, what is stuck in our experience, our lives, our history. The *unknown soldier* comes to mind again. As the quintessence of something that will not end. As if it had become self-evident, as if the past had slipped into the present and cannot be stopped. An obsession unconnected with reality. But it's not only old networks. What else? Perhaps the *unknown soldier* principle is like a vacuum cleaner sucking in people who have something completely different in mind? Is the obsession also a product of obscurantism, resentment, narcissism? I don't know. It's hard, difficult, real. What's with Jacob?

Musk's project of the will. Could it not be essentially a new version of an old idea restyled with the latest technology? A potent relaunch of the hubristic projects of the Cold War? The colonization of Mars. It's Musk's pet idea. In his eyes some kind of move. 'At around $1 million or $500,000 per person, I think it's highly likely that there will be a self-sustaining Martian colony. There will be enough people interested who will sell their stuff on Earth and move. [. . .] If you solve the transport problem, it's not that hard to make a pressurized transparent greenhouse to live in,' says Musk.[63] Peter Thiel, one of the most bizarre characters in Silicon Valley, entrepreneur, venture capitalist, co-founder of PayPal and the first external investor in Facebook, confirms the Musk project: 'It's this going-back-to-the-future idea. There's been this long wind-down of the space programme, and people have abandoned the optimistic visions of the future that we had in the early 1970s. Space X shows there is a way toward bringing back the future.'[64]

Back to the future? A life in transparent greenhouses with controlled atmospheric pressure? Who could want that? Musk would not be Musk if he were put off by such doubts. 'The point is not about me visiting Mars,' he explains, 'but about enabling large numbers of people to go to the planet.'[65] Asked about the temperature of minus 63 degrees on the Red Planet, he replies: 'Eventually you'd need to heat Mars up if you want it to be an Earth-like planet [. . .] and you would have to take real drastic measures with Mars.'[66] The Russian interplanetarists would have said the same thing a hundred years earlier. It was their idea. 'The total mastery and transformation of the universe'.[67] What's the difference?

I'm in the city, navigating from one traffic light to the next. Traffic is sluggish. It doesn't matter. Staying at the wheel, carrying on driving, not getting out. There won't be closure. There isn't any. The sky is new, newer, newest, it is old. Just a few days ago I read an article in the newspaper about the biomedical experiments at Neuralink, a company founded by Elon Musk in 2016 with others with the express aim of developing a brain–computer interface, an invasive neuroprosthesis for the brain. In August 2020 the techno-visionary presented a prototype, a chip 23 mm in diameter and 8 mm thick that was said not only to cure paralysis, Parkinson's, epilepsy, Alzheimer's or vision impairments but also to serve the cyborg plans for the New

Man on Mars. The article didn't mention Mars but was highly critical of the research methods employed by Neuralink.

The US Physicians Committee for Responsible Medicine (PCRM) founded in 1985 filed a suit with the Department of Agriculture against the University of California, Davis.[68] It concerned the chip research on rhesus monkeys commissioned by Neuralink and was based on an almost 600-page document describing the 'disturbing state' of the test animals. 'The documents reveal that monkeys had their brains mutilated in shoddy experiments and were left to suffer and die.'[69] Only eight of the twenty-three test monkeys were still alive. The Physicians Committee noted that the animals had been given a substance known as BioGlue, which destroyed the brain. They had steel posts screwed into their skulls, their skulls were opened as many as ten times, they suffered serious infections, cerebral haemorrhage, facial trauma, seizures and fatal injuries.[70] On 10 February 2022, the PCRM filed a further suit to obtain videos and photos of the research. Both the university and Elon Musk denied the charges. Musk tweeted that chip research on humans was planned for 2022.

I think of the revolution of the Sukhumi monkeys, who paid dearly for their break for freedom. Most of them were shot. The farm was later cleaned up and is today a component of the revived Russian space programme. Intensive virus research on Sukhumi monkeys is reportedly taking place there.

Not only Russia and the USA but above all China is investing in grand orbit dreams. It has defined its planetary ambitions with great precision. It is a long-term strategic project. The first unmanned Moon landing in 2013, the first non-state rocket launch in 2018, landing of a space probe on the far side of the Moon in 2019, permanent manned space station in 2022, solar stations collecting solar energy in the stratosphere from 2023.

Space as a new arena of power politics, as a source of energy and mega-resource for rare earths and precious minerals. Experts believe that there is twenty times more titanium, platinum and above all helium 3 on the Moon than on Earth. Expansionists even speak of the Moon as the 'eighth continent'. Space as a new habitat. The best spots up there are expensive and sought-after. What is history?

It is 15 February 2022. I'm sitting at the kitchen table. The sky above the courtyard has come closer. And this is my report.

Notes

Unknown soldier

1 BArch (Freiburg Military Archive), DVW 2-1/39604, DVW 2-1/39605, DVW 2-1/39606.

2 Hans Haase, 'Studie zur Schaffung von Grundlagen für die Festlegung von Tauglichkeit und Eignung sowie für die medizinische Vorbereitung von Kosmonautenkandidaten der DDR', BArch (Freiburg Military Archive), DVW 2-1/39885, p. 26.

3 See Zentrales Archiv des Deutschen Zentrums; documents unnumbered, no page reference possible.

4 Winfried Papenfuß, 'Der Beitrag des Instituts für Luftfahrtmedizin Königsbrück zur raumfahrtmedizinischen Forschung', Sizungsberichte der Leibniz-Sozietät, Berlin, vol. 96 (2008), p. 97.

5 Haase, 'Tauglichkeit', BArch, DVW 2-1/39885, p. 294.

6 Ibid., p. 27.

7 Ibid., pp. 113 ff.

8 Ibid., pp. 213 ff.

The New Man

1 BArch, Freiburg Military Archive, VA-01/39603, p. 4.

2 Ingmar Bergman, *The Serpent's Egg* (1977), https://subslikescript .com/movie/The_Serpents_Egg-76686.

3 Gerd Koenen, *Utopie der Säuberung: Was war der Kommunismus?* (Berlin, 1998), p. 29.

4 Ibid., p. 28.

5 Boris Groys and Michael Hagemeister, eds., *Die Neue Menschheit: Biopolitische Utopien in Russland zu Beginn des 20. Jahrhunderts* (Frankfurt/M., 2005), p. 41.

6 Ibid., p. 40.

7 Ibid.

8 Ibid., p. 392.

9 Ibid.

10 Ibid., p. 412.

11 Ibid., p. 419.

12 Koenen, *Utopie*, p. 132.

13 Groys and Hagemeister, eds., *Menschheit*, p. 420.

14 Kirill Rossyanov, 'Gefährliche Beziehungen: Experimentelle Biologie und ihre Protektoren', in Dietrich Beyrau, ed., *Im Dschungel der Macht: Intellektuelle Professionen unter Stalin und Hitler* (Göttingen, 2000), p. 348.

15 Ibid.

16 Ibid., p. 350.

17 Ibid.

18 Ibid.

19 Ibid.

20 Ibid., p. 354.

21 Boris Groys, *The Total Art of Stalinism: Avant-Garde, Aesthetic Dictatorship and Beyond*, trans. Charles Rougle (Princeton, 1992), p. 9.

22 Koenen, *Utopie*, p. 145.

Cybernetic lanterns

1 Christoph Mick, 'Deutsche Fachleute in der sowjetischen Rüstungsforschung', in Dietrich Beyrau, ed., *Im Dschungel der Macht: Intellektuelle Professionen unter Stalin und Hitler* (Göttingen, 2000), p. 384.

2 Andreas Malycha, *Biowissenschaften/Biomedizin im Spannungsfeld von Wissenschaft und Politik in der DDR in den 1960er und 1970er Jahren, Beiträge zur DDR-Wissenschaftsgeschichte*, series C, vol. 2, edited by Clemens Burrichter, Gerald Diesener (Leipzig, 2016), p. 42, fn 68.

3 Manfred von Ardenne, *Die Erinnerungen* (Munich, 1990), p. 265.

4 Reinhard Buthmann, *Versagtes Vertrauen: Wissenschaftler der DDR im Visier der Staatssicherheit* (Göttingen, 2020), p. 56.

5 For details of Heinz Barwich's life, see Buthmann, *Vertrauen*, pp. 266 ff.

6 Manfred von Ardenne, BArch, NY 4090/560.

7 Malycha, *Biowissenschaften/Biomedizin*, p. 39.

8 Philipp Aumann, *Mode und Methode: Die Kybernetik in der Bundesrepublik Deutschland* (Göttingen, 2009), p. 89.

9 Stefan Rieger, *Kybernetische Anthropologie: Eine Geschichte der Virtualität* (Frankfurt/M., 2003), p. 30.

10 Aumann, *Mode*, p. 103.

11 *Physik: Lehrbuch für Klasse 11* (Berlin, 1969).

12 Ibid., p. 74.

13 Ibid., p. 132.

14 BArch (MfS), ZAIG 10074.

No admission for unauthorized persons

1 'Innere Ordnung für die Zusammenarbeit der sozialistischen Länder auf dem Gebiet der Erforschung und Nutzung des Weltraumes für friedliche Zwecke', Anlage 2 der Durchführungsanweisung Nr. 1 zum Befehl 2/67 vom 10.1.1967. BArch, ZA, DSt 100503, p. 4.

2 Ibid.

3 Reinhard Buthmann, 'Die DDR im Weltraum: Kosmosforschung im Licht der MfS-Akten', in *Deutschlandarchiv* (1999), no. 2, March/April, pp. 223–32.

4 Zentrales Archiv des Deutschen Zentrums für Luft- und Raumfahrt e.V., Göttingen, BAAR, A874, unnumbered.

5 Ibid., A887, unnumbered.
6 BArch (MfS), ZAGG, no. 338, sheet 4.
7 Zentrale Arbeitsgruppe Geheimnisschutz Abteilung I, 8.7.1980, BArch (MfS), RSt, Abt. XX, no. 754, sheet 3.
8 On the nature of medical training, it says: 'The status of doctors in socialism differs in principle from that of professional colleagues in capitalism and thus also characterizes the socialist awareness of graduates of our universities. While doctors in capitalist societies have an exclusive status alien to the people as a result of narrow-minded and elite thinking, although basically remaining disenfranchised and exploited by capital, in socialism they are bound to the people through their social origins, position, political attitude and method of working, a part of the socialist intelligence', Protokoll 9/72 vom 16.11.1972, BArch (Freiburg Military Archive), DVW 2-1/139602.
9 Ibid.
10 BArch (Freiburg Military Archive), VA-01/39603, p. 4.
11 Torsten Rüting, 'Der Kampf um Pawlows Erbe', in Dietrich Beyrau, ed., Im Dschungel der Macht: Intellektuelle Professionen unter Stalin und Hitler (Göttingen, 2000), p. 325.
12 Ibid., p. 324.
13 Ibid., p. 325.
14 Ibid.
15 Ibid., p. 328.
16 Norman Ohler, Blitzed: Drugs in Nazi Germany, trans. Shaun Whiteside (London, 2016), p. 44.
17 Hans Mommsen, 'Nachwort', in Ohler, Der totale Rausch: Drogen im Dritten Reich (Cologne, 2015), p. 306.
18 Koenen, Utopie, p. 145.
19 Ibid.
20 Haase, 'Tauglichkeit', p. 128.
21 Rüting, 'Kampf', p. 333.
22 Haase, 'Tauglichkeit', p. 126.
23 Ibid., p. 170.
24 Ibid.

25 Ibid., p. 184.
26 Ibid., p. 171.
27 Ibid.

Weightlessness

1 Dwight D. Eisenhower, Farewell Address to the Nation, 17 January 1961, www.youtube.com.

2 Holger H. Herwig, '"One Hell of a Business": The Genesis of the Military-Industrial Complex in the United States', in Dieter H. Kollmer, ed., *Militärisch-Industrieller Komplex? Rüstung in Europa und Nordamerika nach dem Zweiten Weltkrieg* (Freiburg im Breisgau, 2015), p. 29.

3 Egmont R. Koch and Michael Wech, *Deckname Artischocke: Die geheimen Menschenversuche der CIA* (Munich, 2002), p. 100.

4 Ibid., p. 108.

5 Ernst Klee, *Deutsche Medizin im Dritten Reich: Karrieren vor und nach 1945* (Frankfurt/M., 2001).

6 Herwig, 'Hell', pp. 30–1.

7 Ibid., p. 46.

8 Medizinischer Jahresbericht für das Ausbildungsjahr 1964/65, Institut für Luftfahrtmedizin, BArch (Freiburg Military Archive), DVL 4-9/109418.

9 Matthias Uhl, 'Umfang, Struktur und Leistungsvermögen des militärisch-industriell-akademischen Komplexes der Sowjetunion 1945–1970', in Kollmer, ed., *Militärisch-Industrieller Komplex?*, p. 50.

10 Ibid., p. 51.

11 Torsten Diedrich, 'Zwischen Anspruch und Möglichkeit: Die Rüstungsindustrie der DDR', in Kollmer, ed., *Militärisch-Industrieller Komplex?*, p. 179.

12 Ibid., p. 178.

13 Ibid., p. 181.

14 It concerned the development of an infrared seeker, a laser fire-control system for the T-72 tank, an automated mobile command and control system, a missile-bearing fast control boat and the

military use of near-Earth space. In 1982 contracts were signed for an 'optical star sensor' and an 'optical reference unit'. As 'fundamental requirements for space-based missile defence', these devices were among the most secret research projects within East German high technology. They were 'contributions by the GDR to the anti-SDI programme'; quoted from Buthmann, *Vertrauen*, p. 231.

15 Ibid.

Coupling manoeuvre

1 Katharina Hein-Weingarten, *Das Institut für Kosmosforschung der Akademie der Wissenschaften: Ein Beitrag zur Erforschung der Wissenschaftspolitik der DDR am Beispiel der Weltraumforschung von 1957 bis 1991* (Berlin, 2000), p. 27.

2 See *inter alia* Beschluss des Präsidiums des Ministerrates vom 17. 12. 1973 zur Erweiterung des DDR-Beitrages am Interkosmos-Programm der sozialistischen Länder für den Zeitraum bis 1980, BArch (Berlin), DY 30/57747, p. 5.

3 BArch (Freiburg Military Archive), VA-01/39603, p. 6.

4 Jean-Luc Nancy, *Corpus*, trans. Richard A. Rand (New York, 2008).

5 Darstellung der gesellschaftlichen und wissenschaftlich-strategischen Zielstellung eines Forschungsprogramms am Beispiel der Biowissenschaften und naturwissenschaftlichen Grundlagen der Medizin vom 29.8.1973, Archiv der Berlin-Brandenburgischen Akademie der Wissenschaften, Forschungsbereich Kosmische Physik, VFP, 26, 73, 10, sheet 3.

6 Klaus Steinitz, 'The question has often been asked recently whether what we have understood to date as prognosis can now be seen as long-term planning'; Einleitender Vortrag vor dem Vorstand des Forschungsrates zur schrittweisen Entwicklung der langfristigen Planung und die sich daraus ergebenden Anforderungen an die Weiterführung der prognostischen Arbeiten vom 26.6.1972, BArch (Berlin), DF 4/20244, p. 6.

7 Beschluss des Präsidiums des Ministerrates vom 17.12.1973 zur Erweiterung des DDR-Beitrages am Interkosmos-Programm der sozialistischen Länder für den Zeitraum bis 1980, BArch (Berlin), DY 30/57747, p. 5.

8 Buthmann, *DDR*, p. 228.

9 VII. Beratung der Ständigen Arbeitsgruppe der sozialistischen Länder für Kosmische Biologie und Medizin im Rahmen Interkosmos vom 5.–10.5.1974 in Bukarest, SR Rumänien, Zentrales Archiv des Deutschen Zentrums für Luft- und Raumfahrt e.V., Göttingen, BAAR, A857, unnumbered.

10 Zentrales Archiv des Deutschen Zentrums für Luft- und Raumfahrt e.V., Göttingen, BAAR, A857, unnumbered.

11 VII. Beratung der Ständigen Arbeitsgruppe der sozialistischen Länder (see note 9).

12 Zentrales Archiv des Deutschen Zentrums für Luft- und Raumfahrt e.V., Göttingen, BAAR, A850, unnumbered.

13 Herbert Weiz, Konzeption Interkosmos, 17.12.1976, BArch, DF 4/11237, p. 3.

14 Protokoll der Leitungssitzung des Wissenschaftlichen Rates der Militärmedizinischen Akademie vom 11.11.1988, BArch (Freiburg Military Archive), VA-01/39610.

15 Development and assessment of the level of doctoral degrees in 1979: 'All A processes were carried out in the National People's Army Central Hospital. Scientific life was enriched by them and by faculty teaching. . . . Use of the results: five works and their findings were incorporated in the central research project 18, four in central research project 19, and two in central research project 17', Protokoll 5/81 der Fakultätssitzung vom 26.6.1981, BArch (Freiburg Military Archive), DVW 2-1/39601.

16 Protokoll 2/1980 der Fakultätssitzung der Militärmedizin vom 30.1.1980, BArch (Freiburg Military Archive), DVW 2-1, 39605.

17 'Colonel XXX reports that on 15 December 1981, leading comrades of the party and state leadership met to discuss the transfer of military medicine research results to the Academy of Military Medicine', Protokoll 1/1982 der Fakultätssitzung der

Militärmedizin vom 8.1.1982, BArch (Militärarchiv Freiburg), DVW 2-1/39605.

18 'For educational and psychological reasons the number of members of the examination board is to be reduced. Furthermore, the appointment of the chairman of the examination board and the involvement of representatives of the Ministry of State Security and the Ministry of the Interior are to be coordinated', Protokoll der Leitungssitzung des Wissenschaftlichen Rates vom 25.11.1983: Punkt 2.7., BArch (Freiburg Military Archive), DVW 2-1/39606.

19 'The possibilities of collaboration as offered by the Diagnosis and Consultancy Centre for Medical Genetics will be clarified after consultation with the head of the Academy of Military Medicine', Protokoll 1/1982 der Fakultätssitzung der Militärmedizin vom 8.1.1982, BArch (Freiburg Military Archive), DVW 2-1/39605.

20 Protokoll 1/82 vom 14.5.1982, BArch (Freiburg Military Archive), DVW 2-1/39606.

21 Protokoll 1/1982 der Fakultätssitzung der Militärmedizin vom 8.1.1982, BArch (Freiburg Military Archive), DVW 2-1/39606.

22 Zentrales Archiv des Deutschen Zentrums für Luft- und Raumfahrt e.V., Göttingen, BAAR, A823, unnumbered.

23 Ibid.

24 Karl Marx University of Leipzig, Department of Physics, letter of 23 March 1979 to the director of the Central Institute of the Academy of Sciences of the GDR: 'There are no possibilities at present for biological and medical experiments in space in the department's chemical analysis unit.'

Central Institute for Microbiology and Experimental Therapy, Jena, letter of 29 March 1979: 'In reply to your letter of 25 January, I would like to inform you that we are already participating in Interkosmos: characterization of physical stress states of cosmonauts using the ERY test. We cannot offer any more because we are still not clear about the present material.'

Institute for Scientific Information in Medicine, letter of 1 March 1979: 'In your letter of 25 January, you asked for suggestions for biological and medical experiments in space. Unfortunately I am unfamiliar with this subject.' Zentrales Archiv des Deutschen Zentrums für Luft- und Raumfahrt e.V., Göttingen, BAAR, A848, unnumbered.

25 Buthmann, *DDR*, p. 227.

26 BArch (Freiburg Military Archive), DY 30/69607.

27 Ibid.

28 Haase, 'Tauglichkeit', p. 475.

29 Bericht über die Jahreskonferenz der Interkosmos-Arbeitsgruppe Biologie und Medizin vom 28.9.1970–3.10.1970 in Budapest, Zentrales Archiv des Deutschen Zentrums für Luft- und Raumfahrt e.V., Göttingen, BAAR, A867, unnumbered.

30 Ibid.

31 Ibid.

32 Ibid.

33 The substances concerned were mercamine, cystamine, cystaphose, mexamine, prodigiosin, and also ATP (adenosine triphosphoric acid), Zentrales Archiv des Deutschen Zentrums für Luft- und Raumfahrt e.V., Göttingen, BAAR, A867, unnumbered.

34 Ibid.

35 Ibid.

36 Conversation with a woman doctor from Munich, DOH advice centre, 24 March 2016.

37 Conversation with affected GDR prisoners, DOH advice centre, 4 February 2018.

38 Stasi-Treffbericht von Hans-Georg Meier vom 10.11.1976, BArch (MfS), LPZ XX 0001/105, Studien FKS, p. 5.

39 Peter Wensierski, 'In Kopfhöhe ausgerichtet', in *Der Spiegel*, 20/1999.

40 Horst Hoffmann, *Die Deutschen im Weltraum* (Berlin, 1998), pp. 304–7.

41 Abschlussbericht über die Auswertung des Interkosmos-Experiments 'Sprache 1' DDR, p. 2, Zentrales Archiv des Deutschen Zentrums für Luft- und Raumfahrt e.V., Göttingen, BAAR, A848, unnumbered.

42 Zentrales Archiv des Deutschen Zentrums für Luft- und Raumfahrt e.V., Göttingen, BAAR, A848, unnumbered, p. 2.

43 Ibid., p. 11.

44 Ibid.

Abrek and Bion

1 Christiane Baumann, *Die Zeitung 'Freie Erde' (1952–1990): Kader, Themen, Hintergründe – Beschreibung eines SED-Bezirksorgans*, edited by the Landesbeauftragte für die Aufarbeitung der SED-Diktatur (Schwerin, 2013), p. 66.

2 Peter Marx, 'Genosse Journalist', DLF Kultur, Berlin, 1 October 2013.

3 Ibid.

4 José Brunner, *Die Politik des Traumas: Gewalterfahrungen und psychisches Leid in den USA, in Deutschland und im Israel/Palästina-Konflikt* (Berlin, 2014).

5 Ibid., p. 115.

6 Ibid., p. 116.

7 José Brunner, 'Zur Geopolitik des Traumas: Konturen einer kritischen Raumtheorie für die Traumaforschung', in *Trauma und Gewalt*, no. 4, 11/2021, p. 285.

8 'No other conclusion is possible even in those cases in which adult athletes were not informed. The determining criterion is not their age but their ignorance of what they were being given and the associated bodily harm', in Klaus Marxen and Gerhard Werle, eds., *Gefangenenmisshandlung, Doping und sonstiges DDR Unrecht: Dokumentation Strafjustiz und DDR-Unrecht*, vol. 7 (Berlin, 2009), pp. 107–330.

9 BArch (Freiburg Military Archive), DVW 2-1/39604.

10 BArch (MfS), AIM 2696/69-2, p. 45.

11 BArch (Freiburg Military Archive), DVW 2-1/39605.

12 Ibid., DVW 2-1/39860.

13 Ibid., DVW 2-1/40099.

14 Ibid., DVW 2-1/39605.

15 Ibid., DVW 2-1/40189.

16 Ibid., DVW 2-1/39605.

17 Ibid., DVW 2-1/40202.

18 Ibid., DVW 2-1/40305.

19 Ibid., DVW 2-1/39958.

20 'Formation of a space research centre … There were space research enthusiasts but also the attitude: We shouldn't be too ambitious', report by Claus Grote, head of the Koordinierungsrat für Kosmosforschung der DDR, 23 October 1980, BArch (Freiburg Military Archive), DF 4/20253.

21 Hein-Weingarten, *Das Institut*, p. 42.

22 BArch (Freiburg Military Archive), DVW 2-1/39611.

23 Protokoll 1/1982 des Wissenschaftsrates der Militärmedizinischen Akademie, Bad Saarow vom 8.1.1982, BArch (Freiburg Military Archive), DVW 2-1/39606.

24 Protokoll der Plenarsitzung des Wissenschaftlichen Rates der MMA vom 26.11.1982, BArch (Freiburg Military Archive), DVW 2-1/39605.

25 Information on the status of biomedical space research in the GDR in the Interkosmos programme, Königsbrück, 10 September 1981, Zentrales Archiv des Deutschen Zentrums für Luft und Raumfahrt e.V., Göttingen, BAAR, A854, unnumbered.

26 Protokoll der Leitungssitzung des Fakultätsrates der MMA vom 29.4.1983, BArch (Freiburg Military Archive), DVW 2-1/39607.

27 Einladungsschreiben der Akademie der Wissenschaften der DDR vom 5.4.1983, Zentrales Archiv des Deutschen Zentrums für Luft- und Raumfahrt e.V., Göttingen, BAAR, A854, unnumbered.

28 BArch (Freiburg Military Archive), DVW 2-1/39607.

29 Plenarsitzung des Wissenschaftlichen Rates der MMA vom 15.12.1983, BArch (Freiburg Military Archive), DVW 2-1/39607.

30 Protokoll der Fakultätssitzung vom 9.2.1984, BArch (Freiburg Military Archive), DVW 2-1/39607.

31 'Despite the large amount of knowledge and experience of space biology and medicine acquired through manned space travel, biological experiments with unmanned spacecraft are still of great significance (further investigation of biological mechanisms

and reactions in space, revealing of trends, conclusions and fore-
casts for manned space flight)', Zentrales Archiv des Deutschen
Zentrums für Luft- und Raumfahrt e.v., Göttingen, BAAR, A857,
unnumbered.

32 Karl Hecht, 'Zu ersten Ergebnissen des Biosatellitenexperimentes
Kosmos 1514', Bericht an den Koordinierungsrat für
Kosmosforschung der DDR am 29. 5. 1984, Zentrales Archiv des
Deutschen Zentrums für Luft- und Raumfahrt e.v., Göttingen,
BAAR, A823, unnumbered.

33 Ibid.

34 Ibid.

35 Ibid.

36 Ibid.

37 Ibid.

38 Ibid.

39 Ibid.

40 Zentrales Archiv des Deutschen Zentrums für Luft- und
Raumfahrt e.v., Göttingen, BAAR, A854, unnumbered.

41 Ibid.

42 Ibid.

43 BArch (Freiburg Military Archive), DVW 2-1/39603.

Cosmic microwave background radiation

1 'In 1965, by agreement with the commander and command
structure, corvette captain Dr Gürtler was able to obtain from the
military medicine section the necessary new recruits for sports
medicine in the army sport associations. The best and those most
interested in sports medicine were systematically approached',
BArch (Freiburg Military Archive), DVW 2-1/40227, thesis 'Die
Entwicklung der Sportmedizin in der Armeesportvereinigung
Vorwärts', p. 54.

2 Protokoll der Sitzung, Arbeitsgruppe Kosmische Biologie und
Medizin vom 13.11.1981, Zentrales Archiv des Deutschen
Zentrums für Luft- und Raumfahrt e.v., Göttingen, BAAR,
A892, unnumbered.

3 Tätigkeitsbericht von Hans Gürtler im Hinblick auf seine Dissertation B, BArch (Freiburg Military Archive), DVW 2-1/39618.

4 Giselher Spitzer, *Doping in der DDR: Ein historischer Überblick zu einer konspirativen Praxis* (Cologne, 2000), p. 9.

5 Günter Ewert, Rolf Hornei and Hans-Ulrich Maronde, *Militärmedizinische Sektion 1955–1990: Bildungsstätte für Militärärzte, Militärzahnärzte und Militärapotheker an der Ernst-Moritz-Arndt-Universität Greifswald* (Berlin, 2015).

6 'The recruitment is designed to improve work in general with sports medicine at the FKS and to start obtaining more significant operative information from the area of operations, which the candidate should be able to provide as a result of his business travel', BArch (MfS), LPZ AIM 715/86, I, p. 13; Umregistrierung vom GMS zum IMS am 31.5.1976, BArch (MfS), LPZ AIM 715/86, I, p. 13.

7 Report of 29 September 1978, Safeguarding the research project Identification of additional performance reserves for the period 1975–1980: 'The classified state secret concerns the investigation, testing and use of the centrally controlled and monitored substance M to improve the performance of elite athletes in the GDR', BArch, MfS, LPZ AIM 715/86, III, p. 35.

8 BArch (MfS), LPZ AIM 715/86, I/II/III.

9 'The aim of the research commission "Antidotes to chemical agents" from the Ministry of National Defence was to establish antidotes to cyanide poisoning. The research commission was classified as confidential and completed in 1966', BArch (MfS), AIM 2696/69-2, p. 45.

10 BArch (MfS), LPZ Abt. XX 0001/07, p. 36.

11 BArch (MfS), LPZ Abt. XX, FKS, Blatt 225, 19.1.1977.

12 Substance not on the GDR drug list.

13 BArch (MfS), LPZ Abt. XX 0001/10, p. 177.

14 'Es geht um unsere Ehre', *Der Spiegel* 35/91, 25 August 1991.

15 Statement by Prof. Dr. Hansgeorg Hüller on the 'accusations
    made against me', Staatsanwaltschaft Schwerin, 4541 a, 22.1.1993,
    Staatsarchiv Schwerin: 8.33-6/2.

16 'The director of the FKS has instructed that the future defini-
    tion of confidentiality be determined by 13 February 1978 by a
    specially appointed high-level group. Apart from the already clas-
    sified project "Additional performance reserves", all topics and
    projects whose new findings give us a lead in the international
    context are to be examined to determine their confidentiality
    ranking', BArch (MfS), HA XX, 17062, p. 6.

17 'Vorbereitung neuer Staatsaufträge für technisch-technologische
    Durchbrüche in den 90er Jahren', 25 March 1988, Archiv der
    Berlin-Brandenburgischen Akademie der Wissenschaften,
    Bestand Forschungsbereich Geo- und Kosmoswissenschaften,
    Signatur 286, documents unnumbered.

18 'Das Sowjetische Programm zur Erforschung des Weltalls im
    Zeitraum bis zum Jahre 2000: Pläne, Projekte, Internationale
    Zusammenarbeit', Archiv der Berlin-Brandenburgischen
    Akademie der Wissenschaften, Bestand Forschungsbereich Geo-
    und Kosmoswissenschaften, Signatur 217, unnumbered.

19 'The exploration of the biosphere on Mars – whether there is
    or was one – would be an important scientific discovery', 'Das
    Sowjetische Programm', Archiv der Berlin-Brandenburgischen
    Akademie der Wissenschaften, Signatur 217, unnumbered.

20 'The main aim of x-ray astronomy is to diagnose the hot cosmic
    plasma, which occurs in practically all classes of astrophysi-
    cal objects – from the nearest sun-type stars to quasars and
    clusters of cosmologically distant galaxies', 'Das Sowjetische
    Programm', Archiv der Berlin-Brandenburgischen Akademie
    der Wissenschaften, Signatur 217, unnumbered.

21 Planned projects included INTERBOL – exploration of magne-
    tospheric plasma and Sun-Earth relations; APEX – active plasma
    experiments; AKTIVES-IK – cosmic plasma wave laboratory;
    KORONAS – complex near-Earth orbital observations of solar
    activity; PHOBOS – Mars moon Phobos; KOLUMB – near-Mars

orbit; VESTA – gravitation manoeuvre near Mars, 'Das Sowjetische Programm', Archiv der Berlin-Brandenburgischen Akademie der Wissenschaften, Signatur 217, unnumbered.

22 'Das Sowjetische Programm', Archiv der Berlin-Brandenburgischen Akademie der Wissenschaften, Signatur 217, unnumbered.

23 'Extraterrestrial experiments with maximum sensitivity to fluctuations in cosmic microwave background radiation on angle scales from minutes to degrees are designed to obtain information on the recombination of hot and pre-recombination ionized material in space, the amplitude of primary density fluctuations leading to the formation of galaxies, and the nature of hidden mass', 'Das Sowjetische Programm', Archiv der Berlin-Brandenburgischen Akademie der Wissenschaften, Signatur 217, unnumbered.

24 Eberhard Czichon, 'Grundlagenforschung, Kosmosforschung, Forschungsaufgaben, Forschungsorganisation, Akademie der Wissenschaften, UdSSR', Zentrales Archiv des Deutschen Zentrums für Luft- und Raumfahrt e.V., Göttingen, BAAR, A874, unnumbered.

25 Biosatellit 3 was in space from 23 November to 15 December 1975 in cooperation with France and the USA, Zentrales Archiv des Deutschen Zentrums für Luft- und Raumfahrt e.V., Göttingen, BAAR, A857, unnumbered.

26 Karl Hecht, 'Bericht für die Arbeitsberatung der Spezialisten des Instituts für mediko-biologische Probleme des MfG der UdSSR, Moskau, und der Charité der Humboldt-Universität zu Berlin vom 28.10.–2.11.1988 in Moskau', Zentrales Archiv des Deutschen Zentrums für Luft- und Raumfahrt e.V., Göttingen, BAAR, A823, unnumbered.

27 Hecht, 'Arbeitsberatung', Zentrales Archiv des Deutschen Zentrums für Luft- und Raumfahrt e.V., Göttingen, BAAR, A823, unnumbered.

28 'Das Sowjetische Programm', Archiv der Berlin-Brandenburgischen Akademie der Wissenschaften, Bestand

Forschungsbereich Geo- und Kosmoswissenschaften, Signatur 217, unnumbered.

Suitable ground models

1 'Bericht zum Primatenexperiment', Zentrales Archiv des Deutschen Zentrums für Luft- und Raumfahrt e.V., Göttingen, BAAR, A859, unnumbered.

2 'As with all biosatellites, a comparison was made with a synchronous and live experiment on Earth', Zentrales Archiv des Deutschen Zentrums für Luft- und Raumfahrt e.V., Göttingen, BAAR, A823, unnumbered.

3 'Bericht zum Primatenexperiment', Zentrales Archiv des Deutschen Zentrums für Luft- und Raumfahrt e.V., Göttingen, BAAR, A859, unnumbered.

4 Ibid.

5 Ibid.

6 Ibid.

7 Suggestions for Interkosmos programme 1981–1985, letter of the Academy of Sciences of the GDR, 25 May 1981, Forschungszentrum für Molekularbiologie und Medizin, Zentralinstitut für Herz- und Kreislauf-Forschung, Zentrales Archiv des Deutschen Zentrums für Luft- und Raumfahrt e.V., Göttingen, BAAR, A859, unnumbered.

8 Letter of the Academy of Sciences of the GDR, 25 October 1984, Zentrales Archiv des Deutschen Zentrums für Luft- und Raumfahrt e.V., Göttingen, BAAR, A882, unnumbered.

9 Zentrales Archiv des Deutschen Zentrums für Luft- und Raumfahrt e.V., Göttingen, BAAR, A857, unnumbered.

10 Report on the consultations from 25 to 31 December 1986 by specialists of the MDBP and Charité under the bilateral agreement on scientific and technical cooperation, Zentrales Archiv des Deutschen Zentrums für Luft- und Raumfahrt e.V., Göttingen, BAAR, A846, unnumbered.

11 Zentrales Archiv des Deutschen Zentrums für Luft- und Raumfahrt e.V., Göttingen, BAAR, A857, unnumbered.

12 'The topics "development and investigation of substances to increase the stability of the organism under the influence of centripetal acceleration", "dependence of different types of training and the ability of the organism to withstand extreme acceleration" are being processed through the Military Institute for Aerospace Medicine of the People's Republic of Poland.' 'With allowance for the technical capacities of the pharmacological industry of the Hungarian People's Republic, specialists from that country will be consulted on the subject of "tumbling"', Zentrales Archiv des Deutschen Zentrums für Luft- und Raumfahrt e.V., Göttingen, BAAR, A867, unnumbered.

13 Ibid.

14 Ibid.

15 Ibid.

16 Ibid., A823.

17 Ibid.

18 Ibid., A846.

19 Protokoll vom 6.1.1984 der Fakultätssitzung des MMA, Bad Saarow, BArch (Freiburg Military Archive), VA-01/39607.

20 Protokoll vom 9.2.1984 der Fakultätssitzung des MMA, Bad Saarow, BArch (Freiburg Military Archive), VA-01/39607.

21 Bilanz der medizinisch-biologischen Forschungen, Bucharest 1982, Zentrales Archiv des Deutschen Zentrums für Luft- und Raumfahrt e.V., Göttingen, BAAR, A890, unnumbered.

22 The term 'suitable ground models' is taken from the 'Results of the biomedical research conducted in 1981 on Salut 6' in BAAR, A890.

23 BStU, e-mail, 25 February 2020.

24 BStU, letter, 12 March 2020.

25 BStU, e-mail, 24 June 2020.

26 BStU, e-mail, 3 July 2020.

27 BStU, e-mail, 3 July 2020.

28 Statement by the BStU to the public prosecutor's office in Berlin on the investigation of the actions of an unknown person, 4 February 2021, Zeichen 283 UJs 26/21.

29 'Dr Schäker told me on 1 April 1975 that he had given XXX an analysis of the use of hormones to influence performance in competition sport as early as 1968/69. At the time, however, XXX declined to support further work. Dr Schäker nevertheless continued to work on the scientific issues regarding the use of hormones and was requested around 1970 by XXX to submit a further analysis. He gave XXX this analysis and around 1970/71 the work was officially authorized. Since then, experiments have been carried out in the army sports club (gymnastics)', BArch (MfS), LPZ XX 00001/04, p. 6.

30 Report, 30 January 1975, BArch (MfS), LPZ Abt XX 00001/02, p. 4.

31 BArch (MfS), LPZ Abt. XX 0001/07.

32 BArch (Freiburg Military Archive), DVW 2-1/40172.

33 Ibid.

34 Ibid., p. 46.

35 Ibid., p. 45.

36 Gesamteinschätzung 'Zusätzliche Leistungsreserven', Treffbericht von IM Hans-Georg Meier vom 4.7.1979, BArch (MfS), LPZ XX 0001/105, S. 000030, p. 90.

37 Wissenschaftliches Kolloquium am 26./27.11.1981 zum Thema Neuropeptide, BArch (MfS), LPZ Abt. XX 0001/10, p. 14.

38 Argumentationshinweise über die Notwendigkeit der weiteren Beteiligung des TPG Dresden an Aufgaben im Rahmen der Interkosmosforschung, 21.7.1982, Zentrales Archiv des Deutschen Zentrums für Luft- und Raumfahrt e.V., Göttingen, BAAR, A873, unnumbered.

39 Ibid.

40 'Suitable codes are to be devised for the DTSB and the individual associations, the SKS and the SMD. ... All UM application designs are to be destroyed and no new ones accepted', BArch (MfS), LPZ Abt. XX 0001/10, February 1986, p. 149. Or: 'Dr XXX is not to obtain any written documents; everything is to be done orally. The correspondence from VEB Jenapharm is strictly confidential. Substances are to be sent to Dr Schäker directly by

Dr XXX', BArch (MfS), LPZ, Abt. XX 0001/105, Treffbericht
vom 23.7.1979, p. 91.
41 BArch (MfS), LPZ, Abt. XX 0001/10, Bericht vom 3.9.1987,
p. 158.
42 Ibid., Abt. XX 00001/09, Treffbericht IM 'Hans Georgi' vom
5.1.1984, p. 16.
43 Labor Endokrinologie (Schäker), Treffbericht von IM Hans-
Georg Meier vom 1.8.1977, BArch (MfS), LPZ XX 0001/105,
p. 25.
44 BArch (MfS), LPZ, Abt. XX 00001/09, Treffbericht IMS 'Hans
Georgi' vom 5.1.1984, p. 16.
45 Treffbericht IM 'Technik' vom 18.3.1985, BArch (MfS), A637/79,
vol. 3, p. 386.
46 Ibid., p. 410.
47 Bericht zu ersten Ergebnissen des Biosatellitenexperiments
Kosmos 1514 an den Koordinierungsrat für Kosmosforschung
der DDR am 29.5.1984, Zentrales Archiv des Deutschen
Zentrums für Luft- und Raumfahrt e.V., Göttingen, BAAR,
A823, unnumbered.
48 Ibid.
49 Ibid.
50 Aufgabenblatt für Forschung, 16.4.1984, Zentrales Archiv des
Deutschen Zentrums für Luft- und Raumfahrt e.V., Göttingen,
BAAR, A887, unnumbered.
51 Ibid.
52 Ibid.
53 Bodenuntersuchungen, Hypokinese, Zentrales Archiv des
Deutschen Zentrums für Luft- und Raumfahrt e.V., Göttingen,
BAAR, A859, unnumbered.
54 Ibid.
55 Protokoll der Fakultätssitzung der Militärmedizinischen
Akademie, Bad Saarow, vom 24.2.1988, BArch (Freiburg Military
Archive), VA-01/39605.

We are the first

1 Letter to Willi Stoph (chairman of the Council of Ministers of the GDR) from army general Heinz Hoffmann of 8 February 1985, BArch (Freiburg Military Archive), DVW 1/115551, sheet 12.

2 Information vom 20.1.1986 über die Beratung mit Karl Hecht zu seiner Eingabe vom 17.12.1985, Zentrales Archiv des Deutschen Zentrums für Luft- und Raumfahrt e.v., Göttingen, BAAR, A891, unnumbered.

3 'With reference to your letter of 8 February 1985, the Chairman of the Council of Ministers, Comrade Stoph, approves the transfer of responsibility of the Standing Working Group on Cosmic Biology and Medicine to the Academy of Sciences', letter from Herbert Weiz (Deputy Chairman and Minister of Science and Technology) to Heinz Hoffmann, 14 May 1985, Zentrales Archiv des Deutschen Zentrums für Luft- und Raumfahrt e.v., Göttingen, BAAR, A846, unnumbered.

4 Ibid.

5 Ibid.

6 Institut für Wirkstoffforschung: 'Einschätzung der Arbeitsergebnisse im Rahmen des Interkosmos-Programms', Zentrales Archiv des Deutschen Zentrums für Luft- und Raumfahrt e.v., Göttingen, BAAR, A859, unnumbered.

7 Archiv der Berlin-Brandenburgischen Akademie der Wissenschaften, Bestand Forschungsbereich Kosmische Physik, Signatur 225, unnumbered.

8 Sekretariat Weiz, Herbert: Kontrolle zur 'Leitung und Planung von Staatsplanthemen' im Namen von Wissenschaft und Technik, BArch (Freiburg Military Archive), DF 4/20251, p. 2.

9 Letter from the head of the Institute for Space Research to the Academy of Sciences of the GDR of 24 July 1985: 'I have been informed by the Earth and Space Science Research Division that the scientific and technical developments regarding the UV hygrometer and UV radiation intensity and dosimeter are to be shown in September 1985 at the Bezirksmesse der Meister von morgen. . . . The work of the Institute for Space Research was

based on licence agreements. An option agreement was concluded for the UV hygrometer with a West German company and to date 15,000 hard currency marks have been received. As stipulated in the optional agreement, the partners are committed to secrecy. . . . There is a risk that the conclusion of economically favourable licence agreements with the Academy of Sciences could be jeopardized through the undesired and uncontrolled transfer of important technical information and findings', Archiv der Berlin-Brandenburgischen Akademie der Wissenschaften, Bestand Forschungsbereich Geo- und Kosmoswissenschaften, Signatur 160, unnumbered.

10 Volker Hess, Laura Hottenrott and Peter Steinkamp, *Testen im Osten: DDR-Arzneimittelstudien im Auftrag westlicher Pharmaindustrie 1964–1990* (Berlin, 2016), p. 58.

11 Abgeschlossene Vereinbarungen der Militärmedizinische Akademie, Bad Saarow, hier mit der Akademie der Wissenschaften, Zentralinstitut für Anorganische Chemie, BArch (Freiburg Military Archive), DVW 2-1/51511.

12 'The influence of alkyl phosphates on the serum protein and lipoprotein metabolism in experimentally poisoned rats' or 'Animal experiments on the tolerance and efficacy of oxygen-transporting colloidal volume replacement agents', Protokoll der Leitungssitzung des Wissenschaftlichen Rates der Militärmedizinische Akademie, Bad Saarow vom 4.5.1983, BArch (Freiburg Military Archive), DVW 2-1/39607.

13 28/29 September 1989, 5. Saarower Symposium 'Blutreinigung in der Militärmedizin' der AG Detoxikation in Zusammenarbeit mit der HFR 28, BArch (Freiburg Military Archive), DVW 2-01/50511.

14 BArch (MfS) A 637/79, IM 'Technik', part II, vol. 3, pp. 233–8.

15 'UV-Bestrahlung des Blutes', Treff-Bericht 'Egon Miethe' vom 3.12.1982, BArch (MfS), AIM 3220/90, vol. II, p. 303.

16 Letter of 27 May 1982 to the Ministry of Science and Technology, Zentrales Archiv des Deutschen Zentrums für Luft- und Raumfahrt e.V., Göttingen, BAAR A873.

17 IM 'Technik', part II, vol. 3, p. 439, BArch (MfS) A 637/79.

18 The topics: 'Influence of the flow behaviour of blood on oxygen transport capacity', 'Stabilizing in vitro effect on oxygen transport capacity of preserved erythrocytes', 'Modified haemoglobin as oxygen carrier', 'Perfluorinated compounds as oxygen carriers' and 'Hyperbaric oxygenation (according to Ardenne)', BArch (MfS) A 637/79, IM 'Technik', part II, vol. 3, p. 439.

19 Auswertung der 2. Antidopingweltkonferenz Moskau 1989, BArch (MfS), HA XX, no. 939, p. 101.

20 Hess et al., Testen, pp. 236 ff.

21 Bernhard Pörksen and Friedemann Schulz von Thun, Die Kunst des Miteinander-Redens: Über den Dialog in Gesellschaft und Politik (Munich, 2020).

22 Ibid., p. 172.

23 Gerd Machalett, 'Die Doping-Legende', Rubikon, 19 May 2021. At the end of the article there is also a reference by the author to wide-ranging support: 'I am grateful to Henner Misersky for suggestions and pointers in preparing the report. I have not cited his ideas as a source in the text.'

24 Ibid.

25 IM 'Technik', part II, vol. 3, p. 439, BArch (MfS) A 637/79.

26 https://www.bundeswehr.de/resource/blob/52778/b3fa47de385 3904d535da0d9e5c7450/wmm-ausgabe-04-2018-pdf-data. pdf.

27 Gerd Machalett, 'Ein groß angelegter Schwindel?', in RotFuchs, May 2018.

28 Treffbericht von IM 'Technik' vom 16.1.1986, part II, vol. 3, p. 416, BArch (MfS) A 637/79.

29 Ibid.

30 On the GDR health system, see 'Obskure Quellen', in Deutsches Ärzteblatt, 11/2014; on erythrocyte concentrates in GDR blood reserves, see RotFuchs, April 2014; on the warmongering and anti-Russian paranoia, see 'Ein großabgelegter Schwindel?', in RotFuchs, May 2018; on the conspiracy theory surrounding the poisoning of Sergei Skripal, see Junge Welt, 23 October 2020; on

the poisoning of Alexei Navalny, see *Junge Welt*, 16 December 2020.

31 Gerd Machalett publishes in ex-Stasi associations such as the Gesellschaft zur Rechtlichen und Humanitären Unterstützung e.v. and Sport und Gesellschaft e.v., an association of former GDR sports officials with incriminating connections to the Stasi and doping, with the stated aim of 'uncovering the well-funded campaigns to defame GDR sport', and in *RotFuchs*, a magazine founded in 1998 by the German Communist Party Berlin Nordost group, designated by the Saxon State Office for Protection of the Constitution in 2009 as neo-Stalinist and extreme left-wing. *Zeit* journalist Barbara Nolte describes *RotFuchs* as the 'mouthpiece' of former Stasi officers (*Zeit*, 19 July 2006). See also Christian Nestler, 'Zeitschriftenporträt: RotFuchs', in *Jahrbuch Extremismus & Demokratie*, 24/2012, pp. 248–61, esp. p. 261.

32 'Delays in the planned "supporting substances" research project at the FKS could occur on account of the unusually high fluctuation among scientists in the endocrinology laboratory and sports medicine/life science division. The causes and underlying conditions are to be found in problems with the payment, recognition and material motivation of the employees concerned (no possibilities for publication and hence of recognition, minimal or no material motivation)', BArch (MfS), BVfS Leipzig Abt. XX 00042/03, p. 8.

33 Treffbericht vom 16.2.1986, IM 'Technik', part II, vol. 3, p. 416, BArch (MfS), A 637/79.

34 Ibid.

35 Ibid.

36 Ibid.

37 Ibid.

38 'On the significance of changes in blood cells in connection with sideropoenia' (probably a pseudonym, references also to be found in Kreischa and Suhl), Zentrale Fachkommission Sportmedizin, Lehrgang Militärmedizin, BArch, DR 506/2; Spezifische

Aufgaben für die Sportärztliche Hauptberatungsstelle Schwerin für 1990, BArch, DR 506/68.

39 Tobias Voigt and Peter Erler, *Medizin hinter Gittern: Das Stasi-Haftkrankenhaus in Berlin-Hohenschönhausen* (Berlin, 2011), p. 8.

40 BArch (Freiburg Military Archive), DVW 2-1/39940.

41 Ibid.

42 Ibid., DVW 2-1/39958.

43 Ibid., DVW 2-1/40202.

44 Ibid., DVW 2-1/40156.

45 Ibid., DVW 2-1/40305.

46 Ibid.

47 Ibid., DVW 2-1/40203.

48 'Forschung in Haftanstalten "Hinter Mauern": Neue Erkenntnisse zur DDR', in Anna Maria Lehner, *Medizin und Menschenrechte im Gefängnis: Zur Geschichte und Ethik der Forschung an Häftlingen seit 1945* (Bielefeld, 2018), pp. 89 ff.

49 See also Helmut Reichelt, *Die Militärmedizinische Akademie Bad Saarow und ihre Vorgängereinrichtungen, 1954–1991: Ein Bericht aus Dokumenten, Wissen und Erlebnissen* (Berlin, 2016).

50 KP 'Hans' am 19.9.1964, BArch (MfS), 8961/69, p. 39. Stasi department XX/6/1 wrote of Hans Schuster: 'After good contact had been established with Prof. Dr. Schuster in the late 1950s, unofficial contact was inaugurated with him in summer 1964. An unofficial procedure was initiated to organize the cooperation. Because of his position as director of the research department and rector of the DHfK it was not deemed useful to engage him as an IM [unofficial collaborator]', BArch (MfS), XV/958/64, p. 114.

51 Ibid.

52 Ibid., 'The GI recounted that he had had a long meeting in Leipzig on 18 August 1964 with Comrade Minister Mielke. The contact person was highly satisfied with the result of the Leipzig meeting'.

53 MfS-Hauptabteilung XX/6/1, Treffbericht vom 29.7.1965, BArch (MfS): AIM 8961/69, p. 48.

54 'It is particularly important to put the enemy off the scent through sham research facilities, fake results and other measures', GMS 'Hans', BArch (MfS), AGMS 5871/89, p. 48.

55 Spitzer: *Doping*, pp. 1 ff.

56 'Über Aufgaben und Entwicklungstendenzen der Sportmedizin bis etwa 1980', Tonbandabschrift IM 'Philatelist', 28.5.1970, BArch (MfS), HAXX/3, no. 129, sheet 22.

57 Ibid.

58 BArch (MfS), HA XX, no. 17062, p. 7.

59 Ibid.

60 Ibid. The head of the FKS Hans Schuster was able to give more precise details of the 'long-term cooperation'. It involved the Pharmazeutisches Kombinat GERMED in Dresden, VEB-Jenapharm, the Central Institute for Microbiology and Experimental Therapy in Jena, the Central Institute for Isotope and Radiation Protection in Berlin-Buch, the Central Institute for Nuclear Research in Dresden-Rossendorf, the Institute for Clinical Pharmacology of Humboldt University, the Institute for Aerospace Medicine and hence the Military Medicine Academy in Bad Saarow. The research into psychotropic substances from 1984 involved cooperation with the Institute for Substance Research in Berlin, the Paul Flechsig Institute at Karl-Marx University of Leipzig and the Institute for Neuropathophysiology at Humboldt University in Berlin, Treffbericht von GMS 'Hans' am 17.7.1984, BArch (MfS), AGMS 5871/89, p. 206.

61 Letter, Technisch-Physikalischer Gerätebau Dresden to the Academy of Sciences, 3 February 1984, Zentrales Archiv des Deutschen Zentrums für Luft- und Raumfahrt e.V., Göttingen, BAAR, A823, unnumbered.

62 Bericht vom 6.4.1983, BArch (MfS), BVfS Leipzig Abt. XX 00042/03, p. 31.

63 Ibid.

64 BArch (MfS), LPZ Abt. XX 00001/09, pp. 15, 16, 20.

65 Ibid., p. 54.

66 Staatsanwaltschaft Schwerin, 8.33-6/2, 4541-2.

67 IM 'Wolfgang Martinsohn', BArch (MfS), ZAGG, no. 338, sheet 10.

68 Ibid.

69 Kontron Bildanalyse GmbH, Eching bei München; Wintex Instruments GmbH, Mühlheim; Pharmacia LKB Instruments, Vienna; Eppendorf-Nethler-Hinz, Hamburg; Elphymed B. V., Veenendahl; Hewlett-Packard GmbH, Vienna; ICN-Instruments, Northeim, Jäger GmbH u. Co KG, Würzburg; Merck, Darmstadt; Serva-Feinbiochemica GmbH, Heidelberg; Transcommerz, Berlin-West; Boehringer Mannheim GmbH, Mannheim; Beckmann Instruments, Vienna; Rank Xerox London; IHZ, Berlin; Friedrichstraße IIMC Ltd., Oxfordshire; Toshibs, Medical Systems Europe, Berlin-West – BArch (MfS), BVfS Leipzig, Abt. XX 01382, p. 3.

70 Anlage zum Treffbericht IMB 'Technik' vom 20.6.1985, BArch (MfS), A637/79, part II, vol. 30.

71 BArch (MfS), Neubrandenburg AIM, 165/82.

72 Beschuldigtenvernehmung vom 30.10.1997, Staatsanwaltschaft II beim Landgericht Berlin, AZ JS 1014/93, Staatsarchiv Schwerin.

73 Treffbericht IM Hans-Georg Meier vom 10.11.1976, BArch (MfS), LPZ XX 0001/105, p. 5.

74 Ibid.

75 Karl Feller and Bernd Terhaag, 'Pflichten und Verantwortung in der experimentellen Medizin', in Gerhard Burkhardt and Wolfgang Reimann, eds., Aktuelle Rechtsfragen des Arzt-Patient-Verhältnisses (Dresden, 1976), p. 71.

76 Sicherung des Forschungsvorhabens 'Aufdeckung zusätzlicher Leistungsreserven für den Zeitraum 1975–1980', 29.9.1978, BArch (MfS), LPZ XX 0001/105, p.35.

77 Ibid.

78 Gesamteinschätzung Forschung Zusätzliche Leistungsreserven, 1.8.1977, BArch (MfS), LPZ XX 0001/105, p. 30.

79 Ibid.

80 Schwerpunkt Geheimnisschutz, BArch (MfS), HA XX, no. 17062, p. 6.

81 'Wirkungsvergleich verschiedener anaboler Steroide im Tiermodell und auf ausgewählte Funktionssysteme von Leistungssportler und Nachweis der Praxisrelevanz der theoretischen und experimentellen Folgerungen', BArch (Freiburg Military Archive), DVW 2-1/40131.

82 'Untersuchungen zur Beeinflussung des Mischfunktionalen Monooxygenasesystems und des Glutathions-Systems durch körperliche Belastung und Steroide', BArch (Freiburg Military Archive), DVW 2-1/40070.

83 Ibid., p. 8.

84 'Verbesserung des zentralnervalen und neuromuskulären Funktionsniveaus sowie sportartspezifischer Leistungen durch Oxytozin', BArch (Freiburg Military Archive), DVW 2-1/40172, p. 46.

85 'Examinations on the reaction of the organism under sporting stress, illustrated through selected humoral and cellular non-immunological and immunological defence mechanism variables', research carried out in 1986 by the Department of Immunology of the Military Medicine Academy, Bad Saarow. Page 9 of the introduction: 'Defence mechanisms as overall organismic reactions refer here to examinations of defence mechanisms in connection with tumour-host relations conducted in GDR military medical research for over thirty years under the direction of Lieutenant General OMR Prof. Dr. sc. med. Gestewitz. These examinations can also be used as a reference model for determining the reactiveness of the organism under other stress conditions.' Page 18: 'While high doses of exogenous steroids inhibit the humoral and cellular system, a physiological steroid serum level is required for normal immune functions', BArch (Freiburg Military Archive), DVW 2-1/40329. Hans-Rudolf Gestewitz (1921–98) was head of the Central Hospital of the National People's Army in Bad Saarow and later

rector of the Medical Military Academy, also the teacher of army colonel Dr Gerd Machalett.

A thesis defended in Bad Saarow in 1987 was entitled: 'The influence of artificial hypoxia on selected oxygen transport system and metabolism variables in the experimental training of long-distance runners'. It says: 'Adaptability is a characteristic feature of life. . . . At altitude, there is a rapid formation of erythrocytes. . . . From 4,000 metres under intensive stress the cardiovascular system and energy provision are increasingly inhibited', BArch (Freiburg Military Archive), DVW 2-1/40109. At this time, both immunology and hypoxia were originally subjects of Interkosmos research.

86 'Wirkungsvergleich verschiedener anaboler Steroide im Tiermodell und auf ausgewählte Funktionssysteme von Leistungssportlern und Nachweis der Praxisrelevanz der theoretischen und experimentellen Folgerungen', BArch (Freiburg Military Archive), DVW 2-1/40131.

87 Ergebnisse einer klinischen Vorprüfung zur Wirkung von Steroidsubstanzen auf ausgewählte Organfunktionen und auf die physische Leistungsfähigkeit, BArch (Freiburg Military Archive), DVW 2-1/40057.

88 BArch (MfS), LPZ XX 001/105, 22.11.1978, p. 55.

89 Ibid., 24.4.1979, p. 76.

90 Auswertung Treff May, 23.7.1979, BArch (MfS), LPZ XX 0001/105, p. 91.

91 Zwischenbericht Zusätzliche Leistungsreserven, BArch (MfS), LPZ Abt. XX 0001/07, p. 35.

92 BArch (MfS), LPZ Abt. XX 0001/10, p. 147.

93 Ibid., p. 149.

94 Ibid.

95 Ibid. Apart from the required coding, the FKS indicated in February 1986 that the following substances had been investigated: 'Oral Turinabol, STS 646, testosterone propionate, HCG, clomiphene, testosterone enanthate, testotropin, alpha-lipoic acid, B17, piracetam. Substances being tested: precursors, S12,

piracetam, lysine vasopressin, Nivalin, SP, ACTH, opioids', BArch (MfS), LPZ Abt. XX 0001/10, p. 152.

96 Regarding research on civilians at the Military Medical Academy in Bad Saarow: 'Heterogeneity of the doctoral candidates: members of the National People's Army, members of the protection and security bodies, and civilians, insofar as they are studying military medical subjects', Leitungssitzung der Fakultät vom 11.11.1988, BArch (Freiburg Military Archive), VA-01/39610.

97 Krankenakte IG, Sportmedizinscher Dienst, Bezirk Gera (Staatsarchiv Rudolstadt).

98 Hartmut Riedel, 'Zur Wirkung anaboler Steroide auf die sportliche Leistungsentwicklung in den leichtathletischen Sprungdisziplinen', BArch (Freiburg Military Archive), DVW 2-1/40149.

99 Ibid., p. 10.

100 Ibid., p. 3.

101 In an MfS Dresden security concept, it says of Kreischa: 'The central institute of the sports medicine service in Kreischa is the main research centre for sports medicine. . . . The political anti-espionage operations are further qualified by department XX/3 of the Dresden regional administration in coordination with the central confidentiality working group and the Dresden regional administration confidentiality working group', BArch (MfS), HA XX, no. 211, 25.4.1978, p. 15.

Revolution of the apes

1 Achim Thom and Klaus Weise, 'Die Funktion des philosophischen Denkens in der Medizin und die allgemeine Bewegungsrichtung medizinisch-theoretischen Denkens', in Achim Thom and Klaus Weise, *Medizin und Weltanschauung* (Leipzig, 1973), pp. 5–23; Andreas Frewer and Rainer Erices, *Medizinethik in der DDR: Moralische und menschenrechtliche Fragen im Gesundheitswesen* (Stuttgart, 2015); see also Andrea Quitz, *Staat, Macht, Moral: Die medizinische Ethik in der DDR* (Berlin, 2015).

2 Protokoll des Wissenschaftlichen Rates der Militärmedizinischen Akademie Bad Saarow vom 30.1.1991, BArch (Freiburg Military Archive), DVW 2-1/39611.

3 BArch (Freiburg Military Archive), VA-01/39603.

4 Zentrales Archiv des Deutschen Zentrums für Luft- und Raumfahrt e.V., Göttingen, BAAR, A843, unnumbered.

5 Arbeitsbericht vom 25.10.1984, Zentrales Archiv des Deutschen Zentrums für Luft- und Raumfahrt e.V., Göttingen, BAAR, A887, unnumbered.

6 Ibid.

7 Ibid.

8 Kurzinformation und Stellungnahme zu den Fragen vom 14.12.1984. 'Die hier aufgeführten Aktivitäten sind Bestandteil der nationalen Staatsplanaufgabe ZF.06.27 104.50 "Physiologische, biochemische und pharmakologische Prozesse in der Embryonalentwicklung und im adulten Alter unter terrestrischen und kosmischen Bedingungen" und der ZF.06.27 104.59 "Regulator-Peptide und Schlafprofil unter den Bedingungen des kosmischen Langzeitfluges"', Zentrales Archiv des Deutschen Zentrums für Luft- und Raumfahrt e.V., Göttingen, BAAR, A846, unnumbered.

9 Zentrales Archiv des Deutschen Zentrums für Luft- und Raumfahrt e.V., Göttingen, BAAR, A846, unnumbered.

10 Bericht über die Arbeitsberatung der Spezialisten des Instituts für Medikobiologische Probleme des Ministeriums für Gesundheitswesen der UdSSR und den Spezialisten der Charité, Humboldt-Universität im Rahmen des bilateralen Vertrages über wissenschaftlich-technische Zusammenarbeit vom 25.–31.12.1986 in Moskau, Zentrales Archiv des Deutschen Zentrums für Luft- und Raumfahrt e.V., Göttingen, BAAR, A 846, unnumbered.

11 Ibid.

12 Ibid.

13 Ibid.

14 Ibid.

15 Bericht über die Teilnahme an der Beratung der ständigen Arbeitsgruppe sozialistischer Länder für kosmische Biologie und Medizin 'Interkosmos' in Brno/CSSR vom 10.–16.6.1984. Planungen 1986–1990, Zentrales Archiv des Deutschen Zentrums für Luft- und Raumfahrt e.V., Göttingen, BAAR, A825, unnumbered.

16 Ibid.

17 Bericht über die Erfüllung der wissenschaftlichen Forschungsaufgaben des DDR-Teils der Ständigen Arbeitsgruppe der sozialistischen Länder Kosmische Biologie und Medizin im Programm 'Interkosmos' 1987, Zentrales Archiv des Deutschen Zentrums für Luft- und Raumfahrt e.V., Göttingen, BAAR, A859, unnumbered.

18 Untersuchung von Problemen der kosmischen Biorhythmologie unter allgemein-biologischem und psychophysiologischem Aspekt, Zentrales Archiv des Deutschen Zentrums für Luft- und Raumfahrt e.V., Göttingen, BAAR, A859, unnumbered.

19 Ibid.

20 Ibid.

21 Ibid.

22 Ibid.

23 Protokoll der Leitung des Wissenschaftlichen Rates vom 25.11.1983, BArch (Freiburg Military Archive), DVW 2-1/39606.

24 'Das Sowjetische Programm zur Erforschung des Weltalls im Zeitraum bis zum Jahre 2000: Pläne, Projekte, Internationale Zusammenarbeit', Archiv der Berlin-Brandenburgischen Akademie der Wissenschaften, Bestand Forschungsbereich Geo- und Kosmoswissenschaften, Signatur 217, unnumbered.

25 Bericht über die XXI. Beratung der Ständigen Arbeitsgruppe 'Kosmische Biologie und Medizin' der am Programm Interkosmos beteiligten sozialistischen Länder, 6.–11.6.1988, Zentrales Archiv des Deutschen Zentrums für Luft- und Raumfahrt e.V., Göttingen, BAAR, A844, unnumbered.

26 'Leistungsfähigkeit der Frau und ihre Eignung für die militärische Verwendung', BArch (Freiburg Military Archive), DVW 2-1/40189, p. 9.

27 Zentrales Archiv des Deutschen Zentrums für Luft- und Raumfahrt e.v., Göttingen, BAAR, A860, unnumbered.

28 Substanz P-Wirkung auf Reproduktion und Entwicklung gestresster trächtiger Ratten, Zentrales Archiv des Deutschen Zentrums für Luft- und Raumfahrt e.v., Göttingen, BAAR, A859, unnumbered.

29 Untersuchung des Einflusses der Schwerelosigkeit und Hypergravitation auf Wachstum und Entwicklungsprozesse, Zentrales Archiv des Deutschen Zentrums für Luft- und Raumfahrt e.v., Göttingen, BAAR, A859, unnumbered.

30 Zentrales Archiv des Deutschen Zentrums für Luft- und Raumfahrt e.v., Göttingen, BAAR, A843, unnumbered.

31 Ibid.

32 BArch (Freiburg Military Archive), Protokoll der Fakultätssitzung der Militärmedizinischen Akademie Bad Saarow vom 5.9.1996, VA-01/39609.

33 Ibid.

34 Ibid.

35 Ibid.

36 Ibid.

37 Ibid., VA-01/39610.

38 Bericht über die Teilnahme am 8. Symposium der Internationalen Akademie für Kosmonautik vom 29.9.–4.10.1989 in Taschkent, Zentrales Archiv des Deutschen Zentrums für Luft- und Raumfahrt e.v., Göttingen, BAAR, A838, unnumbered.

39 Ibid.

40 Ibid.

41 Ibid.

42 Zentrales Archiv des Deutschen Zentrums für Luft- und Raumfahrt e.v., Göttingen, BAAR, A11246, unnumbered.

43 Projektentwurf Interdisziplinäre Humanwissenschaftliche Weltraumforschung, Zentrales Archiv des Deutschen Zentrums

für Luft- und Raumfahrt e.V., Göttingen, BAAR, A870, unnumbered.

44 Forschungsprojekt 'Kosmische Medizin und Biologie im Interkosmos-Programm', Zentrales Archiv des Deutschen Zentrums für Luft- und Raumfahrt e.V., Göttingen, BAAR, A872, unnumbered.

45 Beratung Ständige Arbeitsgruppe Kosmische Biologie und Medizin, Zentrales Archiv des Deutschen Zentrums für Luft- und Raumfahrt e.V., Göttingen, BAAR, A859, unnumbered.

46 Protokoll der Leitungssitzung des Wissenschaftlichen Rates der Militärmedizinischen Akademie Bad Saarow vom 5.5.1987, BArch (Freiburg Military Archive), VA-01/39609.

47 Ibid.

48 Staatsanwaltschaft Berlin an den Bundesbeauftragten für die Unterlagen des Staatssicherheitsdienstes der ehemaligen DDR vom 7.6.2021, Zeichen: 283 UJs 26/21.

49 Ibid.

50 Gerd Machalett and Helmar Gröbel, 'Der konstruierte Skandal: Behauptungen, im DDR-Sport seien mit Dopingmitteln "Menschenversuche" durchgeführt worden, entbehren jeder Grundlage', in *Rubikon*, 4 August 2021.

51 José Brunner, 'Zur Geopolitik des Traumas: Konturen einer kritischen Raumtheorie für die Traumaforschung', in *Trauma und Gewalt*, no. 4, November 2021, Stuttgart, p. 284.

52 Irena Josifovna Volk, *Die Affen von Suchumi* (Berlin, 1973), p. 6.

53 Sabine Adler, 'Schwerelos in Unterhosen', in Sabine Adler, *Russisches Roulett: Ein Land riskiert seine Zukunft* (Berlin, 2011), pp. 19–23.

Back to the future

1 Arbeitsbuchaufzeichnungen, HA XVIII, Abteilung 5, BArch (MfS), ZA, HA XVIII, nicht erschlossenes Material, Blatt 1–19.

2 Erdmut Wizisla, 'Ausgraben und Erinnern: Walter Benjamins Theorie des Archivierens', in Akademie der Künste, ed., *Arbeit am Gedächtnis* (Berlin, 2021), p. 42.

3 Spitzer, *Doping*, p. 123, fn 2.

4 'Wandlungen der Geburtshilfe nach Einführung der elektronischen Geburtenüberwachung – Eine Vergleichsstudie am Patientengut der Universitätsfrauenklinik der Charité und der Frauenklinik des Zentralen Lazaretts', Protokoll der Leitungssitzung des Wissenschaftlichen Rates der MMA vom 26.3.1980, BArch (Freiburg Military Archive), DVW 2-1/39605.

5 'Über die diagnostische Uringewinnung mittels suprapubischer Blasenpunktion anhand von 600 Punktionen bei Kindern unterschiedlichen Alters', Protokoll der Leitungssitzung des Wissenschaftlichen Rates der MMA vom 14.10.1983, BArch (Freiburg Military Archive), VA-01/39607.

6 'Zur körperlichen und sportlichen Entwicklung von 7 – 9-jährigen schwimmsporttreibenden Kindern', Protokoll der Leitungssitzung des Wissenschaftlichen Rates der MMA vom 26.6.1981, BArch (Freiburg Military Archive), DVW 2-1/39605.

7 Abgeschlossene Vereinbarungen der MMA, Rahmenvertrag 1.12.1986–30.6.1991, BArch (Freiburg Military Archive), DVW 2-1/51511.

8 BArch (Berlin), DY 30/69605, p. 89.

9 Niederschrift 'Beratung über die Abstimmung zum gemeinsamen Vorgehen des Ministeriums für Nationale Verteidigung, PF 98 473 und des Ministeriums für Staatssicherheit, DE 3000 bei der Realisierung des F/E-Vorhabens "Fourieranalysator" vom 22.6.1982', Zentrales Archiv des Deutschen Zentrums für Luft- und Raumfahrt e.V., Göttingen, BAAR, A888, unnumbered.

10 Niederschrift der Beratung über die Einbeziehung einer speziellen Aufgabenstellung aus dem Themenkomplex der Arbeitsgruppe 'Kosmische Biologie und Medizin' in das F/E--Vorhaben 'Fourieranalysator' am 7.4.1982 in der AdW, Abteilung I, Zentrales Archiv des Deutschen Zentrums für Luft- und Raumfahrt e.V., Göttingen, BAAR, A888, unnumbered.

11 Protokoll 'Beratung über die weitere Gestaltung der Beziehungen aller am F/E-Vorhaben "Fourieranalysator" beteiligten Organe/Bereiche der AdW, des MfS und des MfNV am 6.7.1982 in der

AdW', Zentrales Archiv des Deutschen Zentrums für Luft- und Raumfahrt e.v., Göttingen, BAAR, A888, unnumbered.

12 Ibid.

13 Zentrales Archiv des Deutschen Zentrums für Luft- und Raumfahrt e.v., Göttingen, BAAR, A823, unnumbered.

14 Ibid, A860.

15 Ibid., A859.

16 Ibid.

17 Ibid.

18 Ibid., A857.

19 Ibid., A823.

20 Ibid, A852.

21 Ibid.

22 Protokoll der Leitungssitzung des Wissenschaftlichen Rates der MMA vom 8.4.1988, BArch (Freiburg Military Archive), VA-01/39610.

23 Bericht über die Arbeitsberatung der Spezialisten des Instituts für Medikobiologische Probleme des Ministeriums der UdSSR und der Spezialisten der Charité, Humboldt-Universität im Rahmen des bilateralen Vertrages über wissenschaftlich-Technische Zusammenarbeit vom 25.–31.12.1986 in Moskau, Zentrales Archiv des Deutschen Zentrums für Luft- und Raumfahrt e.v., Göttingen, BAAR, A846, unnumbered.

24 Bericht zur Vorbereitung des Biosatellitenexperiments im Rahmen des Interkosmosprogramms in Suchumi vom 20.–29.10.1984. Zentrales Archiv des Deutschen Zentrums für Luft- und Raumfahrt e.v., Göttingen, BAAR, A846, unnumbered.

25 Zentrales Archiv des Deutschen Zentrums für Luft- und Raumfahrt e.v., Göttingen, BAAR, A854, unnumbered.

26 Ibid., A852.

27 Letter from the director of the Central Institute for Cardiovascular Research to the head of the Research Centre for Microbiology and Medicine of 17 December 1982, Zentrales Archiv des Deutschen Zentrums für Luft- und Raumfahrt e.v., Göttingen, BAAR, A852, unnumbered.

28 Ibid.

29 Sektion 'Kosmische Psychologie', Thema 4.12: 'Suche und Vervollkommnung von Methoden zur Bewertung der psychologischen Adaptation des Menschen, anwendbar auf die Bedingungen kosmischer Flüge unterschiedlicher Dauer', Zentrales Archiv des Deutschen Zentrums für Luft- und Raumfahrt e.v., Göttingen, BAAR, A830, unnumbered.

30 Ibid.

31 Protokoll des Wissenschaftlichen Rates der MMA vom 30.1.1991, BArch (Freiburg Military Archive), DVW 2-1/39611.

32 Reichelt, *Die Militärmedizinische Akademie*, p. 72.

33 Ibid., p. 159.

34 Ibid.

35 Ibid., p. 160.

36 Ibid.

37 Jürgen Müller, *Von der Remise des Herzogs zum geheimen Forschungslabor* (Altenburg, 2020), p. 47.

38 Reichelt, *Die Militärmedizinische Akademie*, p. 160.

39 Hein-Weingarten, *Das Institut*, p. 52.

40 Ibid., p. 54.

41 'If there are problems, we are counting on the support of the DARA, since aerospace medicine in the FRG needs to be further developed in general', handwritten comment on a letter by Karl Hecht to the rector of the HU Berlin of 14 June 1991, Zentrales Archiv des Deutschen Zentrums für Luft- und Raumfahrt e.v., Göttingen, BAAR, A838, unnumbered.

42 Hein-Weingarten, *Das Institut*, p. 54.

43 Forschungsprojekt 'Kosmische Medizin und Biologie im Interkosmos-Programm, 1990–1995, Protokoll der 24. Beratung der Ständigen Arbeitsgruppe Kosmische Biologie und Medizin der Teilnehmerländer des Interkosmosprogramms', Zentrales Archiv des Deutschen Zentrums für Luft- und Raumfahrt e.v., Göttingen, BAAR, A872, unnumbered.

44 Protokoll der Arbeitsberatung der Spezialisten des Instituts für Medikobiologische Probleme des Ministeriums für

Gesundheitswesens der UdSSR und dem Institut für Pathologische
Physiologie der Charité der Humboldt-Universität, BRD, im
Rahmen des Vertrages über interinstitutionelle Zusammenarbeit,
15.–22.12.1990, Zentrales Archiv des Deutschen Zentrums für
Luft- und Raumfahrt e.V., Göttingen, BAAR, A838, unnumbered.

45 Ibid.

46 Protokoll der Arbeitsberatung der Spezialisten des Instituts
für Medikobiologische Probleme des MfG der UdSSR und
dem Institut für Pathologische Physiologie der medizinischen
Fakultät (Charité) der Humboldt-Universität, BRD, Moskau,
9.–14.4.1991, Zentrales Archiv des Deutschen Zentrums für
Luft- und Raumfahrt e.V., Göttingen, BAAR, A838, unnumbered.

47 Vorläufige Themenliste gemeinsamer Untersuchungen, Protokoll
der Arbeitsberatung, 9.–14.4.1991, Zentrales Archiv des
Deutschen Zentrums für Luft- und Raumfahrt e.V., Göttingen,
BAAR, A838, unnumbered.

48 Vertrag über wissenschaftlich-technische Zusammenarbeit
zwischen dem Institut für Medikobiologische Probleme
(IMBP) des Ministeriums für Gesundheitswesen der UdSSR,
Moskau, und dem Institut Pathologische Physiologie der
Humboldt-Universität zu Berlin für den Zeitraum 1991 – 1995
zur Problematik: 'Einfluss von extremen Umweltfaktoren auf
funktionelle Zustände von Mensch und Tier', Protokoll der
Arbeitsberatung, 9.–14.4.1991, Zentrales Archiv des Deutschen
Zentrums für Luft- und Raumfahrt e.V., Göttingen, BAAR, A838,
unnumbered.

49 Weitere Information zur zukünftigen Nutzung des Objektes
Gosen, 14.5.1991, Zentrales Archiv des Deutschen Zentrums für
Luft- und Raumfahrt e.V., Göttingen, BAAR, A872, unnumbered.

50 Letter from Karl Hecht to the rector of Humboldt University
Prof. Dr. Fink of 14 June 1991, Zentrales Archiv des Deutschen
Zentrums für Luft- und Raumfahrt e.V., Göttingen, BAAR, A838,
unnumbered.

51 Ibid.

52 Ibid.

53 Ibid.
54 Projektentwurf Interdisziplinäre Humanwissenschaftliche Weltraumforschung. Thema: 'Komplex Verhaltensweisen unter besonderer Beachtung der Psycholokomotorik bei der Beurteilung der psychophysiologischen Stabilität des Astronauten unter langzeitig veränderten Bedingungen', Zentrales Archiv des Deutschen Zentrums für Luft- und Raumfahrt e.v., Göttingen, BAAR, A870, unnumbered.
55 Chronopsycho-Physiologische Untersuchungsmöglichkeiten, Vorhabenbeschreibung, Zentrales Archiv des Deutschen Zentrums für Luft- und Raumfahrt e.v., Göttingen, BAAR, A870, unnumbered.
56 Projektentwurf, Zentrales Archiv des Deutschen Zentrums für Luft- und Raumfahrt e.v., Göttingen, BAAR, A870, unnumbered.
57 Ibid.
58 Ashlee Vance, *Elon Musk, Tesla, SpaceX, and the Quest for a Fantastic Future* (London, 2015), p. 216.
59 Ibid., p. 217.
60 Ibid., p. 15.
61 Ibid., p. 5.
62 Ibid., p. 246.
63 Ibid., p. 333.
64 Ibid., p. 336.
65 Ibid., p. 333.
66 Ibid.
67 Groys and Hagemeister, eds., *Menschheit*, p. 40.
68 'Physicians Group Files States Lawsuit and Federal Complaint Against UC Davis Regarding Deadly Monkey Experiments at Elon Musk-Funded Lab', press release, PCRM, 10 February 2022.
69 Ibid.
70 Ibid.

Bibliography

Adler, Sabine, *Russisches Roulett: Ein Land riskiert seine Zukunft* (Berlin, 2011).

Aumann, Philipp, *Mode und Methode: Die Kybernetik in der Bundesrepublik Deutschland* (Göttingen, 2009).

Baumann, Christiane, *Die Zeitung 'Freie Erde' (1952–1990), Kader, Themen, Hintergründe: Beschreibung eines SED-Bezirksorgans* (Schwerin, 2013).

Bergman, Ingmar, *The Serpent's Egg*, universumfilm, Edition, Disc I (1977).

Bergmann, Anna, *Der entseelte Patient: Die Moderne Medizin und der Tod* (Berlin, 2004).

Beyrau, Dietrich, ed., *Im Dschungel der Macht: Intellektuelle Professionen unter Stalin und Hitler* (Göttingen, 2000).

Brunner, José, *Die Politik des Traumas: Gewalterfahrungen und psychisches Leid in den USA, in Deutschland und im Israel/ Palästina-Konflikt* (Berlin, 2014).

Buthmann, Reinhard, *Versagtes Vertrauen: Wissenschaftler der DDR im Visier der Staatssicherheit* (Göttingen, 2020).

Ewert, Günter, *Interaktionen zwischen der Stadt Greifswald, der Ernst-Moritz-Arndt-Universität und dem Militär* (Berlin, 2007).

Ewert, Günter, Rolf Hornei and Hans-Ulrich Maronde, *Militärmedizinische Sektion 1955–1990: Bildungsstätte für Militärärzte, Militärzahnärzte und Militärapotheker an der Ernst-Moritz-Arndt-Universität* (Berlin, 2015).

Foucault, Michel, *Discipline and Punish: The Birth of the Prison* (New York, 1977).

Frewer, Andreas and Rainer Erices, eds., *Medizinethik in der DDR: Moralische und menschenrechtliche Fragen im Gesundheitswesen* (Stuttgart, 2015).

Goffman, Erving, *Stigma: Notes on the Management of Spoiled Identity* (London, 1990).

Groys, Boris, *The Total Art of Stalinism: Avant-Garde, Aesthetic Dictatorship and Beyond*, trans. Charles Rougle (Princeton, 1992).

Groys, Boris and Michael Hagemeister, eds., *Die neue Menschheit: Biopolitische Utopien in Russland zu Beginn des 20. Jahrhunderts* (Frankfurt/Main, 2005).

Hein-Weingarten, Katharina, *Das Institut für Kosmosforschung der Akademie der Wissenschaften der DDR: Ein Beitrag zur Erforschung der Wissenschaftspolitik der DDR am Beispiel der Weltraumforschung von 1957 bis 1991* (Berlin, 2000).

Hess, Volker, Laura Hottenrott, and Peter Steinkamp, *Testen im Osten: DDR-Arzneimittelstudien im Auftrag westlicher Pharmaindustrie 1964–1990* (Berlin, 2016).

Hoffmann, Horst, *Die Deutschen im Weltraum: Zur Geschichte der Kosmosforschung in der DDR* (Berlin, 1998).

Klee, Ernst, *Deutsche Medizin im Dritten Reich: Karrieren vor und nach 1945* (Frankfurt/Main, 2001).

Koch, Egmont R. and Michael Wech, *Deckname Artischocke: Die geheimen Menschenversuche der CIA* (Munich, 2002).

Koenen, Gerd, *Utopie der Säuberung: Was war der Kommunismus?* (Berlin, 1998).

Kollmer, Dieter H., ed., *Militärisch-Industrieller Komplex? Rüstung in Europa und Nordamerika nach dem Zweiten Weltkrieg* (Freiburg in Breisgau, 2015).

Lehner, Anna Maria, *Medizin und Menschenrechte im Gefängnis: Zur Geschichte und Ethik der Forschung an Häftlingen seit 1945* (Bielefeld, 2018).

Lohl, Jan and Angela More, *Unbewusste Erbschaften des Nationalsozialismus* (Gießen, 2014).

Lovelock, James, *Novacene: The Coming Age of Hyperintelligence* (London, 2019).

Malycha, Andreas, *Biowissenschaften/Biomedizin im Spannungsfeld von Wissenschaft und Politik in der DDR in den 1960er und 1970er Jahren* (Leipzig, 2016).

Marxen, Klaus and Gerhard Werle, eds., *Gefangenenmisshandlung, Doping und sonstiges DDR-Unrecht: Dokumentation Strafjustiz und DDR-Unrecht*, vol. 7 (Berlin, 2009).

Meyer, Sophie, *Immunologie im 'kleinen Staat' DDR: Die tumorimmunologische Grundlagenforschung in Berlin-Buch (1948–1984)* (Berlin, 2016).

Müller, Jürgen, *Von der Remise des Herzogs zum geheimen Forschungslabor* (Altenburg, 2020).

Nancy, Jean-Luc, *Corpus*, trans. Richard A. Rand (New York, 2008).

Ohler, Norman, *Blitzed: Drugs in Nazi Germany*, trans. Shaun Whiteside (London, 2016).

Pörksen, Bernhard and Friedemann Schulz von Thun, *Die Kunst des Miteinander-Redens: Über den Dialog in Gesellschaft und Politik* (Munich, 2020).

Quitz, Andrea, *Staat, Macht, Moral: Die medizinische Ethik in der DDR* (Berlin, 2015).

Reichelt, Helmut, *Die Militärmedizinische Akademie Bad Saarow und ihre Vorgängereinrichtungen, 1954–1990: Ein Bericht aus Dokumenten, Wissen und Erlebnisse* (Berlin, 2016).

Rieger, Stefan, *Kybernetische Anthropologie: Eine Geschichte der Virtualität* (Frankfurt/Main, 2003).

Schleiermacher, Sabine and Norman Pohl, eds., *Medizin, Wissenschaft und Technik in der SBZ und DDR: Organisationsformen, Inhalte, Realitäten* (Husum, 2009).

Schmidtke, Adrian, *Körperformationen: Fotoanalysen zur Formierung und Disziplinierung des Körpers in der Erziehung des Nationalsozialismus* (Münster, 2007).

Spitzer, Giselher, *Doping in der DDR: Ein historischer Überblick zu einer konspirativen Praxis* (Cologne, 2000).

Thom, Achim and Klaus Weise, *Medizin und Weltanschauung* (Leipzig, 1973).

Uhl, Matthias, *Umfang, Struktur und Leistungsvermögen des militärisch-industriell-akademischen Komplexes der Erforschung der Wissenschaftspolitik der DDR am Beispiel der Weltraumforschung von 1957 bis 1991* (Berlin, 2000).

Vance, Ashlee, *Elon Musk, Tesla, SpaceX, and the Quest for a Fantastic Future* (London, 2015).

Virilio, Paul, *L'Art du Moteur* (Paris, 1993).

Voigt, Tobias and Peter Erler, *Medizin hinter Gittern: Das Stasi-Haftkrankenhaus in Berlin-Hohenschönhausen* (Berlin, 2011).

Volk, Irina Josifovna, *Die Affen von Suchumi* (Berlin, 1973).

von Ardenne, Manfred, *Die Erinnerungen* (Munich, 1990).

Index